DIGITAL DEFENSE
ESSENTIAL

A Beginner's Guide to
Cybersecurity and Ethical Hacking
Careers

Robert Williams

TABLE OF CONTENTS

INTRODUCTION

It is impossible to overestimate the critical importance of cybersecurity in the ever-changing digital age, where connectivity and technological advancements have become a part of everyday life. The requirement for skilled people who can protect our networks, systems, and sensitive data has increased to previously unheard-of levels as we negotiate this complex digital landscape. Within this framework, "Digital Defense Essentials" manifests as more than just a book—rather, it is an all-encompassing and illuminating manual designed for novices stepping into the fields of cybersecurity and ethical hacking.

For enthusiasts, beginners, and those thinking about a career in the exciting world of digital security, this guide is more than just a collection of facts; it's a lighthouse that illuminates the road. Carefully addressing a wide range of readers with different degrees of experience, it aims to simplify the intricacies of ethical hacking techniques and cybersecurity principles. Regardless of your level of experience in this fascinating field or your aspirations to become an ethical hacker, this guide is ready to meet you where you are and take you on an intensive, life-changing educational trip.

The field of cybersecurity is characterized by tremendous obstacles, ranging from comprehending the core principles of confidentiality, integrity, and availability to figuring out the advanced methods used by ethical hackers. This guide's chapters are each expertly constructed section that offers a solid foundation for building a strong defense against the ever-changing risks that malevolent actors represent.

This book stands out for its constant dedication to closing the knowledge gap between theory and practice. In addition to teaching theoretical ideas, it provides real-world examples, practical insights, and practical techniques. See ethical hacking in action, learn about the nuances of encryption, and strengthen your digital perimeters with a sophisticated grasp of firewalls. Beyond the technical aspects, though, this guide promotes a holistic viewpoint by exploring the human aspect of cybersecurity, going over the moral conundrums that digital guardians encounter, and highlighting the necessity of ongoing education in this quickly evolving field.

Every chapter reveals a new degree of comprehension and proficiency, much like a key. Not only is knowledge dissemination the aim, but readers will also be equipped with the skills, information, and attitude required to successfully negotiate the many opportunities and problems found in the field of cybersecurity and ethical hacking.

Set off on this educational adventure as "Digital Defense Essentials" clarifies the nuances of digital defense. In order to ensure a safe and robust cyberspace for present and future generations, it extends an invitation to readers to actively participate in safeguarding the digital landscape. Within these pages, information becomes empowering, and curiosity serves as the spark for a fulfilling and significant career in ethical hacking and cybersecurity. Welcome to a world where learning and influence are both intriguing aspects of digital defense, in addition to being a requirement.

CHAPTER ONE

1.0 Definition of Cybersecurity

The word "cybersecurity" acts as a sentinel in the digital age, protecting against the many risks that can be found inside the intricate network of our electronic environments. Cybersecurity is a dynamic science devoted to safeguarding digital systems, networks, and data from harm, unwanted access, and attacks. It is not just a shield.

Fundamentally, cybersecurity is a broad strategy to protect the digital space from a variety of threats, such as malicious software, illegal access, data breaches, and cyber-espionage. It is the proactive endeavor to guarantee information availability, confidentiality, and integrity in the face of constantly changing cyberthreats.

Cybersecurity is not just about protecting individual devices; it's also about protecting whole networks, cloud infrastructures, and integrated systems. It entails putting strong security policies, procedures, and technology in place to guard against potential weaknesses that cybercriminals can exploit.

To put it simply, cybersecurity is the first line of defense against the ever-changing array of cyberthreats that threaten our digital assets, private data, and vital infrastructures. It's a dynamic, ever-evolving area that demands awareness and constant study to keep ahead of enemies attempting to undermine the security of our digital environment. Before we go any farther with "Digital Defense Essentials," it is important to grasp the basic definition of cybersecurity. This will help us as we explore the nuances of protecting the digital frontier.

1.1 Cybersecurity is crucial for newcomers.

Setting up a strong foundation for a safe and powerful online presence is similar to realizing the critical relevance of cybersecurity for novices just starting out in the digital world. The importance of cybersecurity in a society where technology is ingrained in every part of our lives cannot be emphasized.

Personal Data Protection

Defending the Heart of Digital Lives: Our lives are intricately entwined into a complicated web of online activities in the vastness of the digital world. Our digital footprint is a mosaic of our personal information that is created by every financial transaction, social media activity, and digital communication. It is impossible to overestimate the importance of this digital fabric, which makes cybersecurity essential to maintaining the security and integrity of our digital lives.

Knowing Your Digital Tapestry

A multitude of personal data is produced by our digital activities, which include everything from social media posts to online transactions. This includes specifics like financial transactions, contact details, social media connections, and even personal insights about our lives. Our digital fabric serves as a digital archive of our identities on the internet.

Our Digital Footprint's Size

Our digital footprint on the internet goes well beyond what we consciously do. It includes the things we buy, the websites we visit, the material we post, and the platforms we use. This massive data trail creates a digital mosaic that, when assembled, provides a detailed picture of our identities, preferences, and actions.

The Personal Information Vulnerability

This complex digital tapestry conceals our personal information's fragility. This abundance of data can be targeted by malicious actors for a variety of crimes, such as identity theft, financial fraud, or even social engineering attempts. These individuals are frequently motivated by the desire to profit. Strong cybersecurity measures are vital, as evidenced by the possible dangers to personal data.

Cybersecurity as the Magnificent Barrier

In the face of ever changing cyberthreats, cybersecurity proves to be the strong wall separating our private data from those looking to take advantage of it. This complex defensive system consists of a number of tools, procedures, and guidelines intended to guard our online lives from hacking, illegal access, and data breaches.

Strengthening the Digital Stronghold

Encryption is a vital part of this cybersecurity barrier. It protects our private information both during transmission and storage, acting as a virtual fortress. The confidentiality and integrity of our sensitive data are protected by encryption, which converts data into unintelligible code so that, even in the event that it is intercepted, unauthorized parties cannot decode it.

Safe Verification: Guarding Entry Points

By using safe authentication methods, cybersecurity strengthens security. These gatekeeping techniques guarantee that sensitive data and personal accounts are only accessible by those who are allowed. Robust password schemes or sophisticated biometric authentication notwithstanding, safe access turns into a critical component in blocking unwanted access attempts.

Stay Aware and Identify Threats: Alertness in the Digital World

Proactive cybersecurity requires ongoing threat detection and monitoring. Cutting-edge technology actively searches for unusual activity and possible security breaches, such as intrusion detection systems. Cybersecurity serves as a watchful defender, protecting the integrity of our personal data by promptly detecting and eliminating threats.

Creating Awareness and Empowering Users: The First Line of Defense

In the field of cybersecurity, knowledge is a potent tool. Cybersecurity awareness and education programs enable people to identify possible risks, use safe online practices, and actively participate in protecting their personal data. Armed with information, users take on the role of the first line of defense against online attacks.

Maintaining the Digital Soul

Essentially, safeguarding personal data via cybersecurity is a commitment to maintaining people's digital identities in a globalized society, not just a technical requirement. Cybersecurity emerges as the defender of our digital lives, making sure that the minute details of our online personas are safe, unaltered, and faithful to the people they represent through strengthening the digital fortress, putting secure procedures into place, and encouraging a culture of cyber awareness.

1.2 Protecting Digital Assets: Strengthening the Intellectual Property Vault

In today's digital world, both individuals and companies gather a wealth of important resources—creative works, intellectual property, and private information that are the foundation of their efforts. Since these digital assets are the result of strategic planning, ingenuity, and innovation, they are easy prey for hackers and other bad actors looking to gain illegal access, steal, or compromise. As the steadfast defender, cybersecurity is essential to securing the intellectual property vault and guaranteeing the privacy and integrity of these priceless digital assets.

The Variety of Online Resources

The digital era has brought forth a new era when people and corporations produce, store, and manage a wide range of digital assets, going beyond the domain of personal information. These resources include financial information, trade secrets, artistic works, proprietary software, and trade secrets in addition to intellectual property. Every individual possesses inherent worth and builds upon the basis of creativity and achievement.

The Intellectual Property Stakes Are High

Intellectual property includes inventions, trademarks, patents, and copyrights. It is frequently the lifeblood of companies and artists. By acting as a guardian, cybersecurity stops unauthorized parties from stealing or abusing these intellectual assets. Intellectual property protection is essential to maintaining innovation and competitive advantage, in addition to being required by law.

Preserving Artistic Pursuits and Creative Works

Creative people create digital products that reflect their artistic vision and expression, whether they are writers or artists. These artistic creations are protected from digital theft, unauthorized reproduction, and unauthorized access by cybersecurity. Cybersecurity supports the growth of the creative industries and the acknowledgement of creators' rights by safeguarding the integrity of artistic undertakings.

Protecting Private Business Data

Confidential information is essential to business success. Examples include financial data, proprietary algorithms, strategic plans, and customer databases. By creating a secure perimeter around this sensitive data, cybersecurity thwarts attempts by rivals or cybercriminals to obtain illegal access. Ensuring confidentiality in corporate activities is crucial for preserving credibility and gaining a competitive advantage.

Controlling the Potential for Data Breach

Due to the interconnectedness of the digital world, there is a risk of data breaches for enterprises. Strong encryption, access restrictions, and ongoing monitoring are examples of cybersecurity techniques that act as barriers against unwanted breaches. Cybersecurity protects the confidence of customers, partners, and stakeholders whose data is stored in digital repositories by reducing the possibility of data breaches.

Maintaining Data Integrity

The Foundation of Digital Credibility: Integrity is what gives digital assets their value; they have to be genuine and unchangeable. Cybersecurity uses techniques to guard against illegal changes or tampering with digital data, ensuring its integrity. This fundamental component of digital trust is crucial, particularly when working with important operational data, legal documents, or financial records.

Protecting Strategic Information: Countering Cyber Espionage

In a world where strategic information theft is a constant threat due to cyber espionage, cybersecurity becomes an essential line of defense. In order to safeguard national interests and corporate competitiveness, governments, businesses, and other entities of geopolitical importance depend on cybersecurity measures to safeguard their digital assets against industrial or state-sponsored cyber espionage.

Empowering Entrepreneurs and Innovators

Fostering an innovative climate for inventors and entrepreneurs requires them to be able to protect their ideas and creations. These visionaries are empowered by cybersecurity because it offers a safe space for ideation, development, and commercialization. With the knowledge that their digital assets are protected from loss or theft, inventors may concentrate on expanding the realm of what is feasible.

Preserving the Digital Heritage

The cybersecurity field plays a crucial role in protecting digital assets amidst the complex dance of innovation and creativity in the digital environment. Cybersecurity plays a vital role in safeguarding the digital heritage of individuals and businesses by protecting creative initiatives, strengthening the vaults of intellectual riches, and guaranteeing the secrecy of strategic information. By doing this, it creates an atmosphere that protects the benefits of innovation from those looking to take advantage of them or lessen their worth. It is not only technically necessary to secure digital assets through cybersecurity; it is also a commitment to maintaining the integrity and vibrancy of the digital world for future generations.

1.3. Maintaining Digital Privacy: Taking Charge of Personal Areas

The right to privacy is a cornerstone of our digital rights in the wide and interconnected digital world. The necessity for strong safeguards to protect people's digital privacy has been highlighted by the rise in online activity and the expansion of digital platforms. By serving as an empowering force, cybersecurity lowers the likelihood of invasive surveillance, illegal tracking, and other privacy violations by arming novices with the information and tools they need to take control of their digital privacy.

Digital Privacy's Significance

Digital privacy is an essential human right, not just an idea. Maintaining digital privacy is crucial in the online sphere since personal information is frequently exchanged for other goods and services. This goes beyond safeguarding private information to make sure people can use digital platforms without having their personal areas invaded.

The Widespread Use of Internet Monitoring

There are many different types of surveillance in the digital world, including corporate, governmental, and even cybercriminal types. People are frequently under constant observation, from the tracking of online purchases to the collecting of surfing habits. By reducing the hazards associated with widespread surveillance, cybersecurity gives novices the information and resources they need to successfully negotiate this digital maze.

Illegal Monitoring and Profiling

User data collecting and profiling for targeted advertising and other uses has become standard practice. Unauthorized tracking is prevented by cybersecurity measures such as secure communication protocols, anti-tracking software, and browser privacy settings. People can take back control of their online identities by impeding efforts to create comprehensive user profiles.

Securing Channels of Communication

Communication routes have changed in the digital age, bringing with them both convenience and security risks. Cybersecurity guards against interception of emails, texts, and other online correspondence, ensuring the security of digital communications. Ensuring the secrecy of intimate and delicate interactions requires this degree of protection.

Encryption Promotes User Empowerment

The battle for digital privacy has seen the rise of encryption as a potent ally. Learning about cybersecurity enables newcomers to comprehend the function of encryption in protecting data and communications. People strengthen their digital privacy proactively by using encrypted communication tools and safe browsing practices.

Virtual private networks (VPNs) and anonymous browsing

Cybersecurity novices are introduced to tools like virtual private networks (VPNs), which allow them to browse the internet anonymously. By establishing a private, secure tunnel between the user and the internet, these solutions give the user's digital footprint anonymity and disguise it. Comprehending and employing these instruments improves people's capacity to use the web without jeopardizing their privacy.

Securing Individual Devices

Cybersecurity covers personal devices as well, including computers, tablets, cellphones, and other gadgets that hold a lot of personal data. Beginners discover how crucial it is to have strong passwords, biometric authentication, and frequent software updates on their devices in order to prevent unwanted access and possible privacy violations.

Informing Users of the Risks of Social Engineering

Teaching consumers about the dangers of social engineering is a crucial part of protecting their online privacy. Learning about cybersecurity enables novices to identify phishing efforts, social engineering schemes, and other methods used by bad actors to obtain personal data. People can prevent attempts to violate their privacy by using dishonest tactics by being alert.

Confidently Navigating Digital Spaces

Maintaining one's online privacy is a real, actionable right that people can actively defend, not just an ideal. As the facilitator of digital empowerment, cybersecurity gives novices the information, resources, and abilities they need to confidently navigate the digital world. In the rapidly changing digital era, people can restore their right to privacy by taking charge of their personal areas, reducing the likelihood of being watched, and implementing privacy-enhancing behaviors. Digital privacy is a right, not a luxury, that guarantees people the ability to engage in the digital world without violating their personal boundaries. It is protected by cybersecurity measures.

1.4. Protecting Digital Identities Against Exploitation: A Preventive Measure Against Identity Theft

The threat of identity theft looms large in the complex dance of the digital world, where personal information is both necessary and vulnerable. Cybercriminals, skilled at using weaknesses to their advantage, frequently target digital identities since they are valuable assets. For those just starting out, knowing the fundamentals of cybersecurity becomes an essential means of protecting themselves from identity theft, a crime with potentially devastating repercussions if it is successful. As the protector, cybersecurity strengthens digital identities against exploitation and foils identity thieves' cunning plans.

Identity Theft's Threat: Identity theft is a transgression that affects people's daily life on a deeper level than just criminality. Cybercriminals use a variety of methods to steal personal data, including login credentials, bank information, and social security numbers, with the malicious goal of using the victim's identity for fraudulent actions.

Taking Advantage of Vulnerabilities for Malevolent Gains: Cybercriminals use a variety of strategies to take advantage of weaknesses in order to steal identities. Phishing scams, malware assaults, data breaches, and social engineering manipulation are a few examples of these. It becomes essential for novices to comprehend these strategies in order to identify possible dangers and strengthen their digital defenses.

Identity Theft's Aftereffects: Beyond Financial Loss: Identity theft has consequences that go well beyond financial losses. In addition to fraudulent financial transactions and possible compromise of sensitive personal and medical information, victims may experience harm to their credit scores. Having one's identity stolen has a significant emotional cost and can leave a victim feeling violated long after the immediate repercussions have been resolved.

Digital identity protection through cybersecurity: One of the main goals in the field of cybersecurity is to secure digital identities. When novices adopt cybersecurity concepts, they provide a strong barrier against attempts at identity theft. Through proactive measures such as device security and safe online conduct, people can reduce the dangers of identity theft.

Networks and Personal Device Security: Beginner cybersecurity education places a strong emphasis on the necessity of protecting networks and personal devices. Using two-factor authentication, enforcing strong passwords, and updating software are crucial procedures that build defenses against unwanted access. People can prevent attempts to compromise their identity through device vulnerabilities by strengthening their digital perimeters.

Identifying Social Engineering and Phishing Techniques: An essential component of preventing identity theft is identifying the phishing and social engineering strategies that hackers use. Beginners discover how to carefully examine communications, emails, and unsolicited requests for personal data. People can prevent themselves from being victims of fraudulent schemes by cultivating a critical thinking attitude and confirming the authenticity of messages.

Keeping an Eye on Credit Reports and Financial Transactions: Practical precautions like keeping an eye on financial activities and routinely reviewing credit reports are also included in cybersecurity courses. People can discover possible symptoms of identity theft early and lessen the damage on their financial well-being by being alert for suspicious actions and quickly correcting anomalies.

Privacy settings and safe online practices: Identity theft can be prevented in large part by adopting safe online practices, such as modifying privacy settings and exercising caution when publishing personal information on social media. By reducing the exposure of personal information that identity thieves could use against you, cybersecurity enables new users to traverse digital environments with awareness.

Working Together with Credit Monitoring Services: One option for those seeking an extra degree of security is to work with credit monitoring services. These services keep a close eye on credit reports and notify customers of any questionable activity. Credit monitoring services offer an extra layer of protection against identity theft, but they should not be used in place of personal watchfulness.

A Sturdy Guard Against Identity Theft: Cybersecurity appears as the first line of defense in the ongoing fight against identity theft, enabling novices to fortify their digital identities with resilience. By adhering to cybersecurity standards, people not only safeguard their personal data but also help build a digital environment in which identity theft is thwarted as opposed to being an effective exploit. Identity theft prevention is a shared obligation to protect our digital identities in the connected world of the digital age. It is not only an individual responsibility.

1.5. Safe Online Transactions: Taking the Lead in the Digital Marketplace

Ensuring the safety and security of these contacts is crucial in the dynamic digital age where e-commerce and online transactions have become part of everyday life. The fundamentals of cybersecurity function as a barrier, arming novices in the digital economy with the information and resources they need to conduct transactions online safely. Cybersecurity plays a crucial role in ensuring that online transactions are secure, dependable, and convenient by encrypting critical financial data.

How Digital Transactions Have Changed: The rise of internet transactions and e-commerce has revolutionized how people transact business, make purchases, and handle their finances. The ease with which the digital marketplace facilitates transactions—from bill payments and shopping to investing—is unparalleled. But along with this convenience comes the obligation to protect private financial information.

The Dangers of the Online Market: As the online economy grows, so do the hazards involved with conducting business online. Cybercriminals target people's financial information using a variety of strategies, such as phishing, malware, and hacking. For novices, it is essential to comprehend these risks in order to enable them to implement cybersecurity safeguards that protect their private information when doing online transactions.

Transaction Security's Foundation as Cybersecurity Encryption: Cybersecurity encryption is a fundamental practice in online transaction security. To make sensitive data unreadable to unauthorized parties, this method encrypts data, including credit card numbers and personal identifiers. Cybersecurity technologies, such as Transport Layer Security (TLS) and Secure Sockets Layer (SSL), establish a secure data transfer environment, guaranteeing the confidentiality of financial information.

Security of Payment Gateways: A Reliable Route: Cybersecurity provides protection for payment gateways, which are the online channels by which money exchanges. Strong encryption techniques are used by secure payment gateways to protect the integrity of data while it is sent between the user's device and the online service. Beginners discover how to check payment gateway security features to make sure their financial transactions are going through a reliable channel.

Adding an Extra Layer of Security with Two-Factor Authentication: Two-factor authentication is a new security feature in the world of online commerce. It is recommended that beginners activate this function, which usually entails getting a one-time code via a different channel or on a backup device. This guarantees that a second step of verification is needed to finish the transaction, even in the event that login credentials are stolen.

Ongoing Surveillance for Questionable Activities: Cybersecurity requires ongoing surveillance for questionable activity; it is not a one-time task. When people transact online, they learn to check their bank statements frequently, double-check their transaction histories, and report any irregularities or illicit activity right away. Potential hazards can be identified early and mitigated thanks to this proactive strategy.

Informing Users of the Risks of Phishing: Phishing is still a common concern in the digital world, particularly when conducting business online. Novices are instructed on how to spot phishing efforts, stay away from dubious websites, and confirm the legitimacy of emails or messages pertaining to transactions. Users that are aware of cybersecurity issues are better able to discern between authentic messages and fraudulent attempts.

Safe Online Practices for Banking Transactions: The significance of safe browsing practices when doing financial transactions is emphasized by cybersecurity. It is advised that novices utilize trustworthy and safe websites, stay away from using public Wi-Fi for important transactions, and make sure the website's URL starts with "https://" to denote a secure connection. These procedures help create a safer environment for online transactions.

Strengthening Safe Online Transactions: Secure online transactions are protected by cybersecurity principles in the ever-expanding world of digital commerce. Novices can confidently navigate the digital economy by embracing encryption, protecting payment channels, installing two-factor authentication, and adopting watchful behaviors. Not only is it intended to make transactions more convenient, but it also gives people the ability to manage their finances in a trustworthy and safe digital environment. Cybersecurity is a constant ally in the development of the digital marketplace, making sure that the advantages of online commerce are backed by strong protection against possible attacks.

1.6. Protecting Yourself from Cyberthreats: Managing the Digital Age with Cybersecurity Alertness

When novices set out to explore the vast digital world, they encounter a terrain full of varied and constantly changing cyberthreats. The digital frontier presents many problems, ranging from sneaky virus attacks that hide in the virtual shadows to crafty phishing scams that try to deceive. As the lighthouse of defense, cybersecurity awareness equips people with the information and abilities required to not only recognize but also successfully neutralize these threats. Cybersecurity is the defender of a more secure and safe online experience in a world when cyber threats are everywhere.

The Cyberthreats' Dynamic Nature: Cyber dangers take many different forms in the interconnected digital world, and they are always changing and adapting. Phishing assaults use social engineering techniques to trick people, whereas malware looks for ways to get beyond security measures in software and systems. Newcomers to this ever-changing environment must take precautions and be well-informed in order to protect their digital health.

The Danger of Phishing Schemes: Identifying Deceitful Strategies: Phishing scams are a common menace that attempt to trick people into disclosing personal information. Beginners can learn to identify the telltale signs of phishing, such as phony websites, misleading emails, and unsolicited requests for personal information, by learning about cybersecurity awareness. Through honing their capacity to recognize phishing efforts, people can strengthen their defenses against falling for these fraudulent schemes.

Reducing Malware Risks: Strengthening Digital Barriers: Digital security is seriously threatened by malicious software, or malware as it is sometimes called. Cybersecurity gives novices the skills they need to put strong defenses against malware in place. These skills include the significance of using reliable antivirus software, updating software on a regular basis, and being cautious while downloading files or visiting links. Gaining knowledge about malware threats enables people to strengthen their digital defenses against possible attacks.

Safe Online Conduct: The Cornerstone of Cybersecurity: Cybersecurity knowledge highlights the cornerstone of responsible online conduct. New users are taught to use caution when engaging with websites, emails, and texts. A secure digital environment can be created by avoiding clicking on dubious links, confirming the legitimacy of messages, and using caution while disclosing personal information.

Device Hygiene Practices: Protecting Devices Against Cyber Intrusions: Everyday gadgets, such as laptops and cellphones, act as portals to the digital world. The topic of device hygiene is covered in cybersecurity education. This includes setting up biometric authentication, creating strong passwords, and updating operating systems and apps on a regular basis. Novices build a strong defense against possible cyber invasions by safeguarding their gadgets.

Comprehending Social Engineering Techniques: Alertness Against Deception: Cyber risks are largely attributed to social engineering techniques, which use psychological manipulation to trick people. Novices learning cybersecurity awareness are more equipped to identify and foil social engineering scams. Knowing these strategies improves users' awareness of manipulation, whether it is through phone calls, emails, or impersonation.

Two-Factor Authentication Implementation: Strengthening Security Layers: The use of two-factor authentication (2FA) becomes increasingly important as a line of protection against online attacks. Beginners are encouraged to use 2FA by cybersecurity education, which adds an extra layer of verification on top of passwords. Even in the event that login credentials are compromised, this additional step serves as a strong deterrent, preventing unwanted access.

Staying Up to Date with Security Updates: The Dynamic Defense Method: It is essential to stay up to speed on security patches due to the constantly changing nature of cyber threats. Software, programs, and security procedures should be updated on a regular basis, according to cybersecurity advocates. Individuals can guarantee the resilience of their digital defenses against evolving threats by implementing a dynamic defensive method.

Enhanced Defense in the Digital Age: In the face of a constantly changing cyber threat landscape, cybersecurity stands out as the lighthouse that leads novices over the digital wilderness. Cybersecurity enables people to protect themselves from phishing schemes, malware assaults, and social engineering techniques by raising awareness, sharing useful knowledge, and instilling safe online behaviors. It becomes more than just a quest to traverse the digital terrain; those who possess cybersecurity awareness can boldly venture into the wide and linked domains of the digital world. Cybersecurity is the defender of the digital frontier, making sure people can take advantage of its advantages while preserving their digital health in this dynamic and always changing environment.

1.7. Developing Digital Confidence: Using Cybersecurity Assurance to Navigate the Digital Realm

Gaining digital confidence is essential to realizing the linked world's full potential in the ever-changing digital context. It becomes clear that the secret to fostering this confidence and enabling novices to confidently traverse the digital world is a basic awareness of cybersecurity. Equipped with an understanding of cybersecurity, people not only become less vulnerable to online attacks but also acquire the self-assurance necessary to investigate and utilize digital tools and platforms, turning their digital journey into a safe and empowered one.

Digital Confidence's Significance: Beyond just feeling at ease, digital confidence is the conviction that people can interact with the digital environment fearlessly. Building digital confidence becomes a proactive undertaking in an environment where cyber risks are rampant, giving people the skills and mentality they need to fully embrace the advantages of the digital age.

The Function of Cybersecurity Knowledge: An Assurance Foundation: Digital confidence is based on having a solid understanding of cybersecurity. Armed with knowledge of cybersecurity principles, novices are able to comprehend the workings of online threats, encryption techniques, and safe online conduct. This information creates a sense of comfort that opens the door for confident investigation by acting as a barrier against the unknowns of the digital world.

Defensive Edge: Empowering People Against Cyber Threats: Being able to defend against cyberattacks is a vital component of developing digital confidence. People can identify phishing efforts, safeguard their devices, and use safe online practices by receiving cybersecurity education. By encouraging a proactive mindset, this defensive edge enables people to navigate the digital world with resilience against potential risks.

Improving Knowledge of Safe Internet Practices: A Useful Method: Applying safe online practices in real-world situations is essential to fostering digital confidence. Novices acquire knowledge on how to use secure payment methods, create strong passwords, and confirm the legitimacy of websites. These abilities strengthen one's digital security and create an atmosphere in which people can use the internet with assurance and comfort.

Developing an Active Cybersecurity Attitude: The Digital Guardian Way of Thinking: Beyond merely dispensing information, cybersecurity education fosters a proactive attitude. People have a guardian attitude for their digital presence, actively participating in safeguarding it. This proactive strategy, which strengthens digital confidence, entails conducting routine security audits, keeping up with new threats, and adjusting to the dynamic nature of cybersecurity.

Investigating Digital Instruments and Channels: Unveiling Possibilities with Confidence: People with digital confidence can confidently experiment with a wide range of digital tools and platforms. People with an understanding of cybersecurity can use a variety of resources, such as social media networks, e-commerce platforms, cloud services, and online collaboration tools, with confidence because they know how to manage any possible hazards.

An Informed Journey to Embracing the Benefits of the Digital Age: People can enjoy the many advantages of the digital age as their confidence in using technology increases. A cybersecurity-informed journey guarantees that people may completely immerse themselves in the opportunities given by the interconnected world, whether they are working remotely, utilizing digital communication, or using online resources for learning and leisure.

A Safe and Enabled Digital Adventure: Developing digital confidence through cybersecurity education is a transformative process that enables people to move confidently and securely through the digital realm. As novices develop the know-how to protect themselves from online attacks, they take control of their digital future and may confidently explore, connect, and utilize the wealth of resources available in the digital world. Cybersecurity is the lighthouse that points the way to a safe and empowered digital trip in this day and age, when the digital world is an essential component of everyday existence.

For novices, cybersecurity is critical not only for safeguarding personal information but also for bolstering the community's overall resilience on the internet. Understanding and appreciating the value of cybersecurity becomes fundamental as we move through "Digital Defense Essentials," providing a solid foundation on which a safe and secure digital journey can be constructed.

CHAPTER TWO

2.0. Basics of Cybersecurity: The **Structural** Foundations of Digital Defense

The fundamental building blocks of cybersecurity emerge as the dynamic architecture of the digital sphere, influencing the integrity and security of our technological environment. Thoroughly investigating the basic ideas that form the foundation of cybersecurity is crucial as we traverse the intricacies present in this digital realm.

2.1. The CIA Triad, or confidentiality, integrity, and availability, is the foundation of cybersecurity assurance.

The CIA triad—which stands for Confidentiality, Integrity, and Availability—is the fundamental structure that underpins the complex web of cybersecurity principles. These three pillars are more than just theoretical ideas; they serve as the cornerstone upon which strong cybersecurity policies are constructed, guaranteeing the safety, dependability, and accessibility of digital assets. Examining the core of the CIA triangle reveals its importance as the information security compass in the large, networked digital world.

Privacy: Protecting Private Information: Sensitive material is protected by confidentiality, which is the central role of the CIA trio. It guarantees that access to information is limited to those who are permitted, avoiding unapproved disclosure or access. Confidentiality creates a protective perimeter around digital assets by using encryption, access controls, and secure communication protocols to protect the trade secrets that are essential to the survival of people, businesses, and even countries.

Reliability: Maintaining the Pure State of Information: Integrity is the steadfast guardian that guarantees the pure and original state of data. Retaining data's correctness and reliability is crucial in the digital world because it is subjected to multiple transactions and alterations. Integrity acts as a bulwark against attempts to undermine the veracity of digital information by employing strategies like hashing, digital signatures, and version control.

Availability: Guaranteeing Continuous Access to Information and Platforms: Availability appears as the guarantee of continuous access to data and systems in the dynamic and linked digital ecosystem. It guarantees that, when needed, information will be consistently available to authorized users. Robust infrastructure design, redundancy controls, and disaster recovery strategies are all part of availability, which helps to minimize disruptions from unanticipated occurrences, system failures, and cyberattacks. It supports a dependable and seamless digital experience in this way.

The CIA Triad's Interplay: Finding a Balance for Cybersecurity: The CIA triad's power comes from both its individual pillars and from their well-balanced interaction. A thorough cybersecurity strategy must strike a balance between confidentiality, integrity, and availability. For instance, it is essential to preserve the integrity and accessibility of critical data for authorized users while guaranteeing its secrecy. This delicate balance illustrates how cybersecurity is dynamic and how each component supports and enhances the others.

CIA Triad in Practice: Practical Uses: The CIA trinity is used in many different cybersecurity contexts. Organizations use encryption methods in data protection to maintain secrecy. Checksums and digital signatures are two tools used to guarantee the accuracy of data that is transferred. Disaster recovery planning, load balancing, and redundant server setups all help to preserve availability.

Adjusting to Changing Dangers: The CIA Triad's Resilience: Against the constantly changing landscape of cyber threats, the CIA triad remains a flexible and adaptable structure. The guiding concepts of Confidentiality, Integrity, and Availability do not change as technologies progress and threat landscapes evolve. Developing cybersecurity tactics that endure the test of time and new threats requires this agility.

The Significance of Cybersecurity Assurance: The CIA trinity stands out as the personification of assurance in the complex dance of cybersecurity: confidence that information is kept intact, sensitive data is kept private, and access to digital assets is consistently provided. Understanding and adhering to the CIA triad's principles becomes essential to creating a safe and reliable digital environment as people, companies, and societies navigate the digital terrain. The CIA trinity acts as the protector in this dynamic environment where data is a precious resource, making sure that the digital fabric of our globalized society is stitched with the threads of availability, integrity, and secrecy.

2.2. Authentication and Authorization: Cybersecurity's Gatekeepers of Digital Access

The complementary roles of authorization and authentication position them as the watchful gatekeepers at the intersection of digital access in the complex web of cybersecurity. These two essential elements are crucial in strengthening the digital perimeter because they guarantee that only authorized entities are able to access the information and systems.

Examining Authentication and Authorization in greater detail reveals their importance as the defenders of safe access, using cutting-edge tools and techniques to protect digital environments.

Authentication: Precisely Verifying Legitimacy: The first line of security is authentication, which verifies the legitimacy of persons or systems requesting access to digital assets. The digital handshake is the means by which one can ascertain the legitimacy of an entity. The employment of advanced authentication techniques goes beyond simple username and password combinations in the dynamic field of cybersecurity. In order to further increase security and guarantee that only authorized people or systems are granted access, biometric authentication, multifactor authentication (MFA), and adaptive authentication approaches are used.

Biometric Verification: The Accuracy of Distinctive Features: Digital signatures are created by utilizing an individual's distinct physical or behavioral characteristics for biometric authentication. Biometric techniques offer a degree of accuracy that is superior to conventional credentials, ranging from speech patterns and retinal scans to fingerprint scans and facial recognition. Biometrics, acting as a sentinel of authentication, improves security while providing a smooth and intuitive user experience.

Multi-Factor Authentication (MFA): Various Levels of Digital Security: In addition to standard credentials, multi-factor authentication (MFA) adds extra stages of verification to strengthen the authentication process. It frequently combines the user's knowledge (password), possessions (security token), and identity (biometric trait). Using many layers of authentication, each of which poses a different obstacle, MFA acts as a strong defense against unwanted access.

Adaptive Authentication: Real-Time Contextual Vigilance: By taking environmental elements into account in real-time, adaptive authentication gives the authentication process an additional dynamic dimension. It uses a range of analysis parameters, such as device kind, location, and user behavior, to dynamically modify the level of authentication needed. By ensuring that access decisions are in line with the changing risk landscape, contextual vigilance improves security without sacrificing user experience.

Authorization: Precisely Determining Access: Authorization precisely defines the parameters of access, while Authentication opens the gates. By matching digital rights to assigned roles and responsibilities, it makes sure that people or systems can only access the data and features necessary to complete their jobs. Solutions for advanced identity and access management (IAM) are essential for putting granular authorization rules in place and reducing the possibility of unwanted access.

Identity and Access Management (IAM): Coordinating Permissions for Digital Assets: The foundation of authorization is made up of IAM solutions, which manage the intricate dance of digital permits. The administration of user identities, roles, and access controls is centralized using these systems. Organizations can use the least privilege principle by limiting access to persons or systems to what is necessary for their particular jobs through the use of Identity and Access Management (IAM). By reducing the possible consequences of an account compromise, this tactical approach improves security.

Authorization Complexity Streamlining with Role-Based Access Control (RBAC): One of the main components of authorization is Role-Based Access Control (RBAC), which simplifies the intricacy of digital permits. It assigns access permissions to users depending on the preset roles that are created for them based on their responsibilities. RBAC ensures that users in the same role have consistent access rights, making authorization administration easier to handle while preserving a high degree of control.

Ongoing Surveillance and Inspection: Preserving Access Integrity: Authorization and authentication are dynamic processes that need ongoing oversight and inspection. Establishments put in place systems to monitor user behavior, examine access records, and carry out routine examinations to guarantee the accuracy of access restrictions. Maintaining a safe digital environment requires constant attention to detail in order to identify and eliminate possible risks.

Protectors of Digital Access Integrity: In the field of cybersecurity, authorization and authentication work together as the guardians of digital access. When combined, they provide access integrity by confirming the authenticity of entities and specifying the exact details of their digital journeys. Authentication and Authorization remain resilient in the face of developing technologies and dangers as the digital world changes. These gatekeepers perform a symphony of cybersecurity by balancing robust security with user comfort and respecting access integrity principles in the dynamic and interconnected digital world.

2.3. Firewalls and Intrusion Detection Systems (IDS): Using Dynamic Defense to Protect the Digital Periphery

Proactive defenses like firewalls and intrusion detection systems (IDS) develop as dynamic gatekeepers, standing sentinel at the digital border in the unrelenting evolution of the cyber world. These vigilantes for network security use cutting-edge tools like machine learning algorithms and threat intelligence to monitor, manage, and react instantly to possible security risks. Firewalls and intrusion detection systems (IDS) strengthen security measures in the digital sphere by preventing illegal access and potential intrusions.

Firewalls: Network Security's Dynamic Gatekeepers: As the front-runners in network security, firewalls employ a proactive protection mechanism that controls both inbound and outbound network traffic. Modern firewalls go beyond simple packet filtering by utilizing machine learning algorithms and sophisticated threat intelligence. They examine network data closely, identify dangerous tendencies, and decide whether to let or prohibit traffic in real time. By ensuring that only approved and safe communications pass via the network, this dynamic strategy strengthens the defense against cyber threats.

Predicting and Reducing Dangers with Enhanced Threat Intelligence: Advanced threat intelligence is used by firewalls to detect and stop new threats. Firewalls are able to proactively detect possible threats by processing data from several sources, such as known malware signatures, suspicious IP addresses, and behavioral patterns. Firewalls are able to make well-informed judgments, adjust to changing threat environments, and strengthen the digital perimeter with proactive defenses thanks to this intelligence-driven strategy.

Adapting to Dynamic Threats using Machine Learning Algorithms: Firewalls become more adaptive when machine learning techniques are integrated. These algorithms automatically improve decision-making processes by analyzing historical data, seeing trends, and drawing lessons from previous occurrences. Machine learning-equipped firewalls offer a dynamic protection that can identify new threats, detect unusual activity, and adjust in real-time to protect network integrity as cyber attacks become more sophisticated.

Intrusion Detection Systems (IDS): A Continuous Watchdog Over Dangers: Intrusion Detection Systems (IDS) act as a real-time sentinel against potential security threats, complementing the function of firewalls. IDS monitors system and network activity using anomaly detection techniques to spot departures from predetermined norms. IDS provides a quick response to possible security breaches by generating alerts or initiating specified actions when aberrant behavior is discovered.

Algorithms for Anomaly Detection: Identifying Deviations for Quick Reaction: IDS anomaly detection methods are essential for identifying changes from typical network behavior. These algorithms examine past data and network trends to create baselines. IDS generates warnings in response to anomalous activity or possible security risks, enabling cybersecurity professionals to quickly analyze and take appropriate action to lessen the effect of any incursions.

Intelligent Response: Quickly Reducing Dangers: One important advantage of IDS response in real-time threat mitigation is its ability to act quickly. IDS can act quickly to stop abnormal activity by banning particular IP addresses, putting infected devices in quarantine, or inciting incident response procedures. By addressing possible attacks before they have a chance to escalate, this quick response capability improves the overall resilience of network security.

Synced Defense: IDS and Firewalls Working Together: IDS and firewalls frequently cooperate to create a coordinated defense plan. Firewalls use pre-established rules and threat intelligence to actively control network traffic; intrusion detection systems (IDS) add extra levels of protection by spotting possible threats that might evade conventional defenses. By working together, the security posture is improved overall and a thorough, multi-layered defense against various cyberthreats is created.

Ongoing Observation and Adjustment: The Vigilant Watchers: Systems like firewalls and intrusion detection systems are always watching and learning. They develop in tandem with new cyberthreats, guaranteeing the continued efficacy of security measures against changing attack techniques. Maintaining the robustness of the digital perimeter and adapting to the ever-changing cyber landscape require this constant vigilance.

Adaptive Protection for the Digital Era: Intrusion Detection Systems and firewalls stand out as the reliable defenders of the digital perimeter in the dynamic and always changing cyber scene. By utilizing cutting-edge technologies and prompt response capabilities, their proactive defenses establish a strong barrier against any potential invasions and unauthorized access. The collaborative efforts of firewalls and intrusion detection systems (IDS) serve as a crucial pillar supporting network security as enterprises negotiate the intricacies of the digital frontier. This ensures that the digital domain is protected from the numerous threats that lurk in the digital shadows.

2.4. Encryption: Using the Art of Secure Communication to fortify digital fortresses

The complex methods of encryption algorithms represent the peak of information security in the constantly changing field of cybersecurity. One of the strongest foundations of digital defense is encryption, which uses strong cryptographic techniques to convert sensitive data into ciphertext—a complicated and unintelligible code. Encryption assumes the role of the protector of integrity and secrecy in the complex dance of cybersecurity, making sure that data is safe and hidden from unauthorized parties' prying eyes. Notably, the development of encryption methods that are resistant to quantum mechanics offers an additional degree of security in protecting data from possible risks associated with quantum computing.

Sturdy Cryptographic Techniques: The Key to Encryption Power: The use of strong cryptographic techniques is the foundation of encryption. These techniques, which are frequently based on mathematical algorithms, make it possible to convert plaintext data into ciphertext. The robustness and intricacy of these algorithms determine how strong encryption is. Contemporary encryption algorithms, such Rivest Cipher (RSA) and Advanced Encryption Standard (AES), are reliable tools in the cybersecurity toolbox that offer a strong foundation for protecting confidential data.

Data Conversion: From Plain to Cipher: The original, understandable form of data, known as plaintext, is changed into an encrypted, unintelligible form known as ciphertext throughout the encryption process. Cryptographic keys are complicated character sequences that are used by encryption techniques to enable this transformation. The recipient can reverse the process and return the ciphertext to its original plaintext form by using the associated decryption key. Safe communication routes are built on this complex dance of encryption and decryption.

Privacy: Protecting Information from Unauthorized Views: The main goal of encryption is to maintain confidentiality. Encryption assures that even if unauthorized parties intercept the data, they will be unable to decrypt its contents without the matching decryption key because it converts data into ciphertext. When sending sensitive data across networks, this cryptographic shield becomes especially important since it guards against eavesdropping and illegal access.

Reliability: Preventing Tampering: Encryption is essential for maintaining data integrity in addition to confidentiality. A subset of encryption methods known as cryptographic hash functions produce fixed-size hash values or checksums that are particular to given datasets. Recipients can confirm the integrity of the received data by comparing these values. Any illegal changes or tampering with the ciphertext become visible, making it possible to quickly identify possible security breaches.

Analyzing Quantum Threats using Quantum-Resistant Encryption Algorithms: With the development of quantum computing, the possibility of cracking conventional encryption techniques appears closer. As a result, quantum-resistant encryption methods are embraced by cybersecurity. These state-of-the-art cryptographic methods are built to resist quantum computers' processing capability, which has the ability to break conventional encryption. Sensitive data stays safe in the quantum era thanks to quantum-resistant algorithms like hash- and lattice-based cryptography, which strengthen digital fortifications against new threats.

A Look Ahead at Post-Quantum Cryptography: A phrase that encompasses quantum-resistant algorithms, post-quantum cryptography, provides an insight into the future of encryption. This developing topic investigates alternate cryptography techniques that withstand advances in quantum technology. The pursuit of post-quantum cryptography techniques emphasizes cybersecurity's dedication to remaining on top of developments and proactively countering new threats.

Use in Diverse Industries: From Finance to Communication: Encryption is used in many different fields, including secure communication routes, financial transactions, and healthcare data. Encryption protects critical transactions in the financial domain and guarantees the integrity and confidentiality of financial data. Encryption protects patient data and medical information in the healthcare industry, maintaining privacy and adhering to legal requirements. Encryption is a key component of secure communication channels, such as virtual private networks (VPNs) and encrypted messaging apps, which provide private, impenetrable means for information sharing.

The Key to Cybersecurity Resilience is Encryption: Encryption is the keystone that strengthens digital castles against possible attacks in the cybersecurity symphony. Encryption protects sensitive data's secrecy and integrity by strategic use of strong cryptographic techniques and quantum-resistant algorithms that foresee future developments. Encryption remains resilient in the face of changing digital landscapes, adjusting to new threats and reinforcing its role as a pillar of the continuous effort to achieve cybersecurity resilience.

2.5. Security Guidelines and Protocols: Developing Cyber Resilience via Flexible Governance

The creation of a robust security posture in the complex field of cybersecurity depends on the careful creation and execution of extensive security rules and procedures. Cyber resilience is based on these dynamic frameworks, which are maintained by advanced governance, risk management, and compliance (GRC) solutions. Security policies and procedures, which are proactive defenses against changing threats, are embodied protocols, best practices, and standards. Moreover, these frameworks are elevated by the incorporation of machine learning (ML) and artificial intelligence (AI) algorithms, which allow for constant evolution and adaptation in the face of shifting cybersecurity environments.

All-encompassing Security Guidelines: The Cyber Resilience Blueprint: The fundamental guidelines that specify an organization's cybersecurity strategy are its security policies. These documents give forth the general expectations, rules, and principles pertaining to the protection of digital assets. Comprehensive security policies offer a road map for building an environment that is resistant to cyberattacks, covering everything from data protection and access controls to incident response and staff knowledge.

Institutional Structures: Converting Directives into Practice: Procedural frameworks convert security policies into operational procedures, whereas security policies establish the overall strategic direction. Procedures outline the methodical approaches to putting security measures in place, making sure that the intentions of policies are translated into actual implementation. By creating a uniform and standardized approach to cybersecurity procedures throughout the company, this procedural layer promotes a strong protection against any threats.

Risk management, compliance, and governance (GRC): guaranteeing effectiveness and adherence: The implementation of governance, risk management, and compliance (GRC) solutions is essential to the upholding of security rules and procedures. These products offer a well-organized structure for planning and managing cybersecurity projects. Risk management assesses and reduces possible dangers, governance sets up the leadership and monitoring framework, and compliance guarantees adherence to legal obligations. When combined, GRC solutions support the methodical implementation of security measures and promote an environment that is both effective and compliant.

Ongoing Development via AI and ML: Flexible Structures for Changing Environments: The emergence of machine learning (ML) and artificial intelligence (AI) has brought about a radical change in security protocols. These cutting-edge tools analyze data trends, spot anomalies, and instantly respond to new threats, all of which help cybersecurity frameworks continue to evolve. Through proactive detection and reaction, AI and ML algorithms improve the agility of security measures and help enterprises stay ahead of developing cyber threats.

Behavioral Analytics: Revealing Patterns Instantaneously: In the field of behavioral analytics in particular, AI and ML algorithms are essential for real-time danger detection. These algorithms create baseline behaviors for systems, networks, and individuals so they can quickly spot irregularities that can be signs of possible security breaches. By taking a proactive stance, companies can minimize the effect of incidents by being able to respond quickly to emerging threats.

Predictive Analysis: Forecasting Potential Dangers: Predictive analysis is made possible by the integration of AI and ML into security policies. In this process, computers evaluate past data to foresee and get ready for potential threats. Organizations can close possible vulnerabilities before they are exploited by implementing preventative steps thanks to this forward-looking capacity. As a proactive defensive strategy, predictive analysis matches security protocols to the dynamic threat landscape.

Adaptive Response: Improving Security Instantaneously: AI and ML support systems for adaptive response to changing cyber threats. With the use of these technologies, security frameworks can optimize defenses and make autonomous adjustments in response to real-time threat intelligence. Adaptive response builds resilience against new threats by ensuring that security measures continue to be effective in the ever-changing cyber ecosystem.

Programs for Training and Awareness: Developing a Cyber-Aware Culture: Security policies cover the human aspect through training and awareness initiatives; they go beyond paperwork and procedures. These programs train staff members on incident response procedures, threat awareness, and cybersecurity best practices. Organizations can empower their workforce to actively participate in ensuring a safe environment by cultivating a cyber-savvy culture.

Adaptive Governance to Enhance Cyber Resilience: Security policies and processes, which guide enterprises toward cyber resilience, are the cornerstone of dynamic governance in the dynamic landscape of cybersecurity. These frameworks are elevated by the integration of AI and ML technologies, which make proactive threat identification, adaptive response, and ongoing evolution possible. The proactive creation and dynamic enforcement of security policies, which help organizations navigate the intricacies of the digital age, are evidence of the dedication to cybersecurity resilience—a dedication that reaches from strategic leadership to each and every person who helps to protect digital assets.

2.6. Increasing Security Knowledge and Training: Developing the Human Factor in Cyber Defense

In the constantly changing field of cybersecurity, information becomes a powerful tool in the fight against online dangers. Fundamental cybersecurity concepts include the crucial human component in addition to technological ones. Building up the defense against cyber attacks requires constant training and the cultivation of a security-aware culture. By employing state-of-the-art technologies like virtual reality (VR) and augmented reality (AR), companies give users the information and abilities they need to identify and address possible threats, turning them into active contributors to the collective effort of cyber defense.

The Significance of the Human Element in Cybersecurity: The human factor is still essential to preserving a safe digital environment, even in the face of sophisticated technologies and strong protocols. Human weaknesses are frequently exploited by cyber threats, therefore it's critical to provide people with the skills and information needed to properly traverse the digital world.

Security Awareness: Developing an Attitude of Cyber-Resilience: Security awareness is an attitude that penetrates every part of a business and goes beyond the conventional concept of cybersecurity. It entails giving every person in the company, from executives to front-line staff, a thorough awareness of the possible risks and hazards. Security awareness campaigns increase public understanding of the value of cybersecurity and foster a sense of shared accountability for protecting digital assets.

Ongoing Training: Maintaining Competence Against Changing Threats: In the ever-changing field of cybersecurity, continuous training is essential to maintaining current and sharp skills. People are kept up to date on the newest cyberthreats, attack techniques, and security best practices through regular training sessions. These initiatives encourage a proactive approach to cybersecurity that goes beyond simple compliance by enabling users to adjust to new problems.

Application of AR and VR Technologies: Immersion Education for Practical Readiness: Incorporating virtual reality (VR) and augmented reality (AR) technologies into cybersecurity training is a paradigm change. These immersive technologies immerse users in lifelike simulations of surroundings and offer interactive experiences that resemble actual cyberthreats. Through regulated and secure environments, people may practice navigating scenarios like malware infections, social engineering attempts, and phishing attacks with AR and VR training modules.

AR in Security Education: Increasing Interactivity and Realism: By superimposing digital data over the real world, augmented reality adds realism and engagement to security training. By simulating circumstances in which users receive phishing emails, augmented reality applications can help users spot warning signs and make wise judgments. This participatory method improves the capacity to identify and react to possible attacks while fostering a deeper awareness of cybersecurity principles.

Virtual Reality for Detailed Cybersecurity Models: Through the creation of fully replicated settings, virtual reality enhances the immersive experience. Users can tour virtual workspaces, come across phishing attempts, and practice safe behaviors in VR cybersecurity scenarios. Users can hone their cybersecurity abilities in a secure and regulated environment by using this hands-on method in a virtual setting, which will ultimately increase their resilience to actual threats.

Gamification: Adding Interest and Reward to Education: Initiatives for security awareness and training frequently use gamification to enhance and enrich learning.

Challenges, tests, and prizes are examples of gamified components that turn training into an engaging and entertaining activity. Organizations can improve user engagement and motivation by including game-like elements into cybersecurity education. This can create a culture where people actively strive to improve their cyber hygiene.

Ongoing Evaluation and Input: Customizing the Educational Process: Developing security awareness and training should be an ongoing process rather than a one-time event. A customized learning experience is facilitated by ongoing evaluation, individualized feedback, and focused interventions depending on each learner's progress. With this strategy, users are certain to get the help and direction they require to gradually improve their cybersecurity expertise.

Encouraging People to Be Cyber Defenders: The development of security awareness and continual training becomes a strategic necessity in the field of cybersecurity. Organizations that acknowledge the value of human interaction enable people to take an active role in the group's defense against cyberattacks. Training programs are elevated by the incorporation of AR and VR technologies, which offer immersive experiences that contribute to real-world readiness. Establishing a security-aware culture within a business makes every person a cyber defender, strengthening the digital ecosystem's resilience against a constantly changing threat landscape.

2.7. Patch Management: Preventive Defense to Protect the Digital Ecosystem

Proactively managing software vulnerabilities is crucial for preserving a robust cybersecurity posture in the dynamic digital economy. This requirement is met by patch management, a strategic element that makes sure software and systems are updated and patched on a regular basis. Organizations can quickly find and fix known vulnerabilities by utilizing sophisticated automated solutions, which are frequently driven by AI-based vulnerability scanners. This tactical approach reduces the possibility of being exploited by bad actors looking to take advantage of software flaws while simultaneously strengthening the digital infrastructure.

The Digital Ecosystem's Dynamic Nature: An Appeal for Preemptive Defense: The digital ecosystem is dynamic by nature, with new technologies emerging quickly and developments being made on a constant basis. A similar difficulty brought up by this dynamism is the identification of software and system vulnerabilities. Proactive defense systems are necessary to offset this. Patch management is a proactive approach that quickly fixes vulnerabilities and protects the digital environment from any attacks.

The Update Process Can Be Streamlined Using Automated Patch Management Solutions: Manual patching, particularly in intricate digital infrastructures, can be a laborious and time-consuming process. By streamlining this procedure, automated patch management solutions help businesses update and patch software across their networks more effectively. These technologies shorten the window of exposure to possible attacks by automatically identifying vulnerabilities and applying patches using sophisticated algorithms.

AI-Powered Vulnerability Scanners: Improving Identification and Repair:

AI-powered vulnerability scanners are essential to patch management effectiveness. These cutting-edge solutions scan networks and systems for potential vulnerabilities using artificial intelligence. Through the use of machine learning algorithms, these scanners are able to identify new risks in addition to established vulnerabilities. This flexibility guarantees a more thorough protection against potential exploits and improves vulnerability identification's overall efficacy.

Daily Updates: Shutting the Vulnerability Window: The routine updating of systems and software is the foundation of patch management. Organizations are required to rapidly implement the patches that developers release to remedy vulnerabilities in order to seal any potential security gaps. Frequent updates reduce the chance of cyber adversaries exploiting the system and guarantee that it is resilient against known threats.

Proactive Cyber Defense: Quick Mitigation of Known Vulnerabilities: The quick mitigation of known vulnerabilities is one of patch management's main benefits. Organizations can apply updates to address vulnerabilities as soon as they are discovered. This proactive strategy improves the overall security posture by drastically reducing the window of opportunity that bad actors have to take advantage of vulnerabilities.

Minimizing Potential for Exploitation: Reducing Attack Surface: Reducing the attack surface, or potential weak places in a system, is one of the benefits of effective patch management. Organizations reduce chances of exploitation by swiftly resolving vulnerabilities that have been identified. This decrease in the attack surface improves the organization's resistance to cyber assaults while also bolstering the general security of digital assets.

Aligning with Best Practices through Integration with Cybersecurity Frameworks: Patch management is a crucial component of best practices and larger cybersecurity frameworks. It is consistent with the tried-and-true defense-in-depth theory, in which several security tiers cooperate to produce a strong defense posture. Patch management is integrated into cybersecurity frameworks to guarantee a comprehensive and all-encompassing strategy for digital defense.

Ongoing Surveillance and Adjustment: Changing in Line with the Threat Environment: The threat landscape is constantly changing as new vulnerabilities appear and cybercriminals modify their strategies. Patch management needs to be continuously monitored and adjusted. It is imperative for organizations to be attentive and utilize AI-driven scanners to rapidly identify and address emerging dangers. This ongoing cycle of observation and adjustment guarantees the organization's resilience in the face of a constantly evolving world of digital threats.

Empowering People in the Environment of Digital Defense: As we examine the nuances of patch management, it becomes evident that this procedure is essential to empowering people in the context of digital defense and goes beyond simple technicality. Novices with a technological bent who are knowledgeable about patch management actively contribute to the overall robustness of the digital environment. Through comprehension and use of these fundamental cybersecurity architectural pillars, individuals may play a crucial role in strengthening the digital infrastructure and safeguarding against constantly emerging cyber threats.

During our exploration of the fundamentals of cybersecurity, these architectural pillars help novices who are interested in technology navigate the complex world of digital defense. Equipped with this understanding, people may actively contribute to the overall resilience of the digital ecosystem in addition to being able to understand the complexities of cybersecurity.

2.8 Crucial Terms: Deciphering the Complexities of Cybersecurity Terminology

2.8.1. Malware: The Changing Face of Cyber Threats

The term "malware," which is a portmanteau for "malicious software," describes a broad and ever-changing spectrum of online hazards. This umbrella phrase encompasses a wide range of malicious types, each with their own set of skills to compromise, damage, or take advantage of digital equipment, networks, and data. Ransomware, worms, trojans, viruses, and spyware are all members of the large family of malware, each with unique traits and modes of operation.

Viruses: Transform Attachments into Authentic Applications: One of the most common types of malware is a virus, which infiltrates normal systems covertly. These hostile entities insert their malicious code into software that is unaware of its presence, much like biological viruses. Viruses spread by attaching to other programs once they are enabled, which may be harmful to digital ecosystems.

Worms: Autonomous Propagation via Networks: Because of their self-sufficient proliferation, worms are a type of malware that may move freely throughout networks. Worms can spread without the assistance of host applications, unlike viruses. Because of their ability to replicate itself, they can spread throughout networks and take advantage of weaknesses, which makes them especially dangerous and difficult to contain.

Trojans: Deceitful Masks in Authentic Software: Trojans, who take their name from the myth of the ancient Greeks, enter systems by posing as trustworthy software. Under the pretense of reliable applications, trojans trick users into unintentionally installing them. Once inside, they compromise system security and integrity by releasing their malicious payloads.

Ransomware: Data Encryption for Coercive Extortion: A frightening kind of virus known as ransomware seeks to extort users in exchange for the release of encrypted sensitive data. Users are prevented from accessing their own data by this coercive method until a ransom is paid. Attacks using ransomware frequently target people, companies, and even vital infrastructure, requesting cryptocurrency payments in order to avoid detection.

Spyware: Secret Gathering of Private Data: Spyware operates surreptitiously, concentrating on obtaining private data without the user's awareness. This covert type of malware records keystrokes, keeps tabs on user activity, and gathers personal information. Following collection, the data is used maliciously for a number of reasons, such as financial fraud, identity theft, or unapproved monitoring.

Protective Techniques: Sturdy Antivirus, Frequent Updates, and User Education: It needs a complex strategy to defend against the diverse terrain of malware. As a first layer of security, strong antivirus software actively detects and neutralizes dangerous entities. Frequent upgrades, including system and software patches, strengthen weaknesses and block possible malware entry sites. User education is equally important since it enables people to identify and neutralize possible threats in an efficient manner, creating a human barrier against the various strategies that malware uses.

It becomes critical to comprehend the subtleties of malware and implement thorough defensive techniques in the complex field of cybersecurity. This basic understanding prepares tech-savvy novices to actively contribute to the overall resilience of the digital ecosystem and successfully traverse the ever-changing virus landscape as they set out on the path of digital defense.

2.8.2. Phishing: Cracking the Code of Deceptive Manipulation:

Phishing is a sophisticated sort of social engineering in which cyber attackers use deceptive tactics to trick people into disclosing highly sensitive information. This dishonest artistry can take many forms, such as well constructed websites that look reliable or emails that are sent to the wrong person. The principal aim is deceiving users into voluntarily divulging confidential information, financial details, or login credentials.

Spear Phishing: Accurate Targeting: Spear phishing is a technique used in phishing that takes manipulation to a more focused level. Attackers that use spear phishing modify their dishonest strategies to target particular people or companies. Precision targeting frequently includes investigating the target's personal or professional background, which increases the phishing attempt's convincingness and difficulty in identifying it.

Vishing: Voice Communication Manipulation: Vishing is a type of phishing where the main manipulation method is voice communication. Attackers trick people into giving sensitive information by using phone calls or voicemails. Vishing uses social engineering techniques over voice channels in an attempt to take advantage of people's weaknesses and obtain private information through what appears to be genuine contact.

Defense Techniques: Providing Users with Authority, Email Filtering, and Advanced Authentication: To counter the complex risks posed by phishing, a multifaceted security strategy is required. User education is a fundamental tenet that enables people to identify the telltale indicators of phishing efforts and use caution while interacting with others online. As a first layer of security, strong email filtering systems recognize and stop phishing emails before they get to the user. A further line of protection is added by using sophisticated authentication techniques like multi-factor authentication (MFA), which demand more than just passwords to gain access.

2.8.3. Zero-Day Vulnerability: Experiencing the Unknown World of Cyberthreats

A Zero-Day Vulnerability is a serious security hole in hardware or software that hackers take advantage of before the manufacturer fixes it. The phrase "Zero-Day" emphasizes how urgent the matter is because it means that the vulnerability is used the moment it is made public. Users are exposed and vulnerable to possible vulnerabilities because of this immediacy until the software or device provider takes corrective action.

The Race Against Time: Zero-Day Exploitation Dynamics: Attackers and defenders are in a race against time due to the dynamics of zero-day vulnerabilities. Armed with information about a vulnerability, cyber adversaries take quick advantage of it in an effort to extend the window of opportunity before a patch is created and made available. Conversely, users have no days of protection against prospective threats during this interim time, leaving them in a vulnerable state.

Avoiding the Unseen: Proactive Security Measures: Proactive security measure implementation is necessary for the effective management of Zero-Day Vulnerabilities. Both individuals and organizations need to implement tactics that foresee the unknown and reduce potential hazards before they arise. Continuous monitoring, threat hunting, and vulnerability assessments are all part of this proactive approach to find and fix such weaknesses before they are taken advantage of.

Threat Intelligence: Providing Light on the Cyber Environment: It becomes clear that threat information is essential to controlling zero-day vulnerabilities. Organizations can shed light on the cyber landscape by remaining up to date on the most recent cyber threats, vulnerabilities, and attacker strategies. With this information, defenders can better prepare for possible Zero-Day exploits and react more quickly and efficiently when a new vulnerability is discovered.

Quick Reaction Techniques: Reducing Exposure to Exploits: Rapid response techniques are essential when dealing with Zero-Day Vulnerabilities. When a vulnerability is found, organizations need to have systems in place that allow them to quickly develop and implement fixes or mitigations. This quickness in reacting lowers the window of opportunity for possible exploitation, lowering the possibility of a large-scale effect.

Working Together and Sharing Information to Strengthen Collective Defense: Since Zero-Day Vulnerabilities could have a large-scale impact and are urgent, information exchange and cooperation among cybersecurity experts are critical.

Strengthening the collective defense against Zero-Day exploits involves exchanging threat knowledge, attack patterns, and mitigation measures. This cooperative strategy improves the overall resilience of the digital ecosystem.

2.8.4. Firewall: Vigilantly Protecting the Digital Periphery

A firewall is a reliable protector in the ever-changing digital landscape. It plays a vital function in keeping an eye on and managing all network traffic, both coming in and going out. This virtual sentinel creates an impenetrable barrier between trusted external networks and dangerous attackers by operating according to established security standards.

Network Firewalls: Connectivity's Guardians: The network firewall is one example of this digital guardian in action; it is a sentinel stationed at the intersection of internal and external networks. The network firewall acts as a gatekeeper, carefully inspecting each data packet that passes across the network. It compares these packets to pre-established security rules and decides whether to allow or prohibit communication depending on predetermined standards. It is essential to use this strategic control mechanism to combat future cyberattacks and illegal access attempts.

Intelligent Firewalls: Protecting Specific Devices: Host-based firewalls safeguard specific devices in addition to the entire network. These device-centric guardians enforce access control policies that are customized to meet the specific security requirements of each system by analyzing traffic at the level of individual computers or devices. Incorporating host-based firewalls into a multi-layered protection system offers an extra line of defense against possible intrusions and data breaches.

Digital Fortification Blueprint Creation: Access Control Policies: Access control policies are the foundation of firewall operation; they are like a carefully drawn plan for an online defense. The rules that determine whether circumstances allow or prohibit network traffic are set forth in these regulations. Firewalls protect the digital perimeter from potential dangers by enforcing these policies, which guarantee that only authorized entities pass through the digital gates.

Data Packet Analysis: Deciphering the Complexities of Information Flow: Firewalls constantly examine the data packets that are moving over the network. This thorough examination entails looking over each packet's content, determining its source and destination, and determining whether or not it complies with set security regulations. Firewalls are able to detect and eliminate possible threats before they have a chance to infiltrate the well guarded perimeter thanks to this diligent inspection.

Preliminary Protection Against Unauthorized Entry: Strengthening Cybersecurity Foundations: Firewalls act as the first line of protection against illegal access attempts, acting as a digital bastion. These guardians prevent hostile entities from infiltrating internal networks by continually monitoring and managing network traffic. In addition to preventing unwanted access, this proactive defense posture serves as a cornerstone for the larger cybersecurity environment.

A Sentinel's Duty: Protecting Against Cyber Attacks and Data Breaches: A firewall's function goes beyond controlling access; it actively defends devices and networks from online threats and possible data leaks. Firewalls contribute to the overall security posture by identifying and blocking harmful traffic, protecting digital assets' confidentiality, integrity, and availability.

2.8.5. Encryption: Mathematically Accurate Protection of Digital Secrets

The mathematical protector of digital secrets is encryption, which uses a transformation mechanism to change plaintext into ciphertext. By ensuring the safe transfer and storage of sensitive data, this cryptographic technology strengthens information integrity and secrecy in the digital sphere.

Mastering the Art of Transformation with Cryptographic Algorithms: A library of intricate cryptographic algorithms forms the basis of encryption. These algorithms use encryption keys as their artistic tools, combining the power of mathematics with accuracy. When it comes to encoding and decoding data, encryption keys play a crucial role. They enable a safe dance that converts readable plaintext into an impenetrable layer of ciphertext and vice versa.

A Mutual Secret Dance in Symmetric Cryptography: Using a shared key, symmetric cryptography creates a symphony of secrecy. The same secret key is utilized in this dance of encryption and decryption to encode and decode data. Symmetric cryptography is a reliable option for safeguarding large volumes of data in a variety of digital transactions because of its simplicity and speed.

Elegant Ballet of Key Pairs in Asymmetric Cryptography: A pair of keys—the public key and the private key—take center stage in the graceful ballet of asymmetric cryptography. While the private key is kept a closely-guarded secret, the public key is shared freely. Data confidentiality and integrity are improved by a security ballet that results from the fact that information encrypted with the public key can only be decoded with the matching private key.

Quantum-Resistant Encryption: Getting Ready for Computing's Quantum Leaps: Quantum-resistant encryption techniques gain prominence as the digital world prepares for the possibility of quantum computing. These cutting-edge cryptographic techniques are made to withstand the possible dangers posed by quantum computers, guaranteeing that data integrity and secrecy will hold true even in the face of exponential increases in processing capacity.

Data Security Role: Protecting Against Unauthorized Accessors: In the digital world, encryption is essential to protecting data from unauthorized access. It creates a strong defense against prying eyes and possible cyber enemies by encrypting important data. Secure and private data is protected whether it is in transit or at rest thanks to encryption.

Protecting Privacy in the Digital Age: An Essential Obligation: Fundamentally, encryption carries out the essential responsibility of protecting privacy in the digital sphere. It promotes confidence in the naturally linked and information-driven world by enabling people, organizations, and systems to interact and trade safely.

2.8.6. Using Two-Factor Authentication (2FA) to Authenticate in New Ways

By adding an extra degree of protection to conventional authentication techniques, Two-Factor Authentication (2FA) stands out as a sentinel at the forefront of digital access. By requiring users to give two different authentication factors, this dynamic defense technique creates a strong barrier against potential unwanted access.

A Dynamic Pair of Security: The Two Authentication Factors: The fundamental component of 2FA is the demand that users provide two authentication factors, which makes the authentication process more robust and difficult. The initial factor usually consists of something the user is already familiar with, like a password, which serves as a fundamental key to access. A tangible component, such as a temporary code sent to a mobile device, is introduced by the second factor. The authentication procedure is strengthened by the dynamic security duo of knowledge and possession.

Biometrics: An Unique Identity Signature:
Contemporary 2FA systems go beyond
conventional approaches by utilizing
cutting-edge strategies like biometrics. Unique
physical or behavioral characteristics, such as
speech patterns, facial features, or fingerprints,
are used as the second element in biometric
authentication. An additional degree of security
is added by this intrinsic and individualized
feature of identification, which guarantees that
access is only granted to authorized users who
possess the proper biological signature.

**Time-Based Tokens: An Adaptable Security
Protocol:** Time-based tokens give two-factor
authentication a temporal component. The
second factor in this implementation is a code
that is updated on a regular basis. The
time-based nature of these tokens improves
security by decreasing the window of
opportunity for possible attackers. The code,
which is frequently produced by a mobile app
or a dedicated device, corresponds with the
idea of "something the user possesses."

**Smart Cards: A Tangible Key to Virtual
Worlds:** The combination of digital and
physical security is embodied by smart cards.
These tangible cards serve as the second

factor in 2FA and are frequently incorporated with a microcontroller. To authenticate, users insert or tap the smart card, which combines the advanced technology of integrated chips with the conventional possession factor. For added protection against unwanted access, digital domains come with a physical key.

Reducing Vulnerabilities in Single-Factor Authentication: Increasing Security Resilience: One of the strongest defenses against the weaknesses of single-factor authentication is two-factor authentication (2FA). It greatly lowers the possibility of illegal access brought on by compromised credentials or passwords by forcing users to supply two different factors. It is especially important to protect critical accounts or systems from the constantly changing cyber threat landscape with this enhanced security resilience.

Helping to Maintain System and Account Security: An Essential Component of Digital Defense: 2FA makes a big difference in account and system security in the complicated world of digital defense. It is an essential component of the complex strategy for safeguarding digital assets and sensitive data.

With two more layers of security added to authentication, two factor authentication (2FA) gives consumers more confidence to navigate the digital world knowing that their access points are protected from unwanted intrusion.

2.8.7. Reaction to Event: Coordinating Accuracy in Cybersecurity Fallout

In the tumultuous aftermath of a cybersecurity event, incident response steps in as the choreographer of order. This methodical and thorough process entails a painstaking dance of incident identification, containment, eradication, recovery, and analysis. The ultimate objective is not only to recover but also to reduce damage, reduce risks in the future, and strengthen resistance to the constant stream of new and emerging dangers.

The Incident Response Five-Step Dance

Identifying Incidents: Prior to the performance, possible incidents are identified. This entails constant observation, the ability to spot anomalies, and quick identification of any warning indicators of a possible breach or security vulnerability.

Resisting the Danger: As soon as a danger is discovered, the response team acts quickly to contain it, stopping future growth and minimizing possible harm to systems and digital assets.

Taking Out the Primary Cause: After containment is accomplished, attention turns to eliminating the incident's underlying cause. This entails a careful examination, evaluation, and removal of the weak points or compromised components that caused the breach.

Restoring Digital Equilibrium: After eradication, recuperation comes into focus. Restoring impacted systems, data, and services to their original state is the goal of this phase. The goal is to get things back up and running while making sure the digital environment is protected from future occurrences of this kind.

Continuous Improvement Analysis: The incident's analysis, dissection of its complexities, and learning from the experience comprise the last act. This post-event study strengthens the organization's overall cybersecurity posture and aids in ongoing improvement by improving incident response procedures.

The Orchestra of Event Reaction Strategies: This coordinated reaction is played out using incident response plans as the sheet music. These plans include coordinated efforts, communication methods, and clearly defined procedures to guarantee a prompt and efficient response. Regular simulations are used to hone the symphony's coordination and preparedness for the unpredictable nature of real-world events.

A Proactive Approach to Cybersecurity: Facilitating Continual Improvement: Beyond only responding to problems, incident response encourages proactive cybersecurity practices. Organizations can enhance their ability to respond to present problems and strengthen their defenses against potential threats by undertaking routine simulations and comprehensive post-incident analyses. Every event is guaranteed to act as a trigger for enhancing the overall cybersecurity posture thanks to this cycle of continuous development.

Efficient Arrangement and Exchange of Information: The Conductor's Baton: For incident response to be effective, prompt coordination and unambiguous communication are essential. The response team is the conductor, bringing various parties together to work harmoniously. By keeping lines of communication open and honest, everyone may work together to lessen the effects of the incident.

Building a Culture of Cyber-Resilience: The Capstone: The development of a cyber-resilient culture is the ultimate objective of incident response, not merely recovery. Organizations that are adept at incident response not only bounce back from problems quickly, but they also emerge from them stronger, more adaptable, and more ready to take on the ever-changing cybersecurity threat landscape.

2.8.8. Penetration Testing: The Journey of Ethical Hacking Into Cybersecurity Domains

Penetration testing, often known as ethical hacking, is a proactive cybersecurity technique in which security experts replicate a cyber expedition while imitating the strategies of malevolent actors. Finding flaws and vulnerabilities that attackers attempting to gain unauthorized access might exploit is the obvious goal. Various testing approaches, such as white-box, black-box, and gray-box, weave a story in this coordinated investigation that gives enterprises deep insights into the strength of their security posture.

The Craft of Digital Battlefields: The Art of Simulated Cyber Attacks: Penetration testing is essentially the art of building a controlled digital battlefield. Equipped with their skills in ethical hacking, security experts simulate cyberattacks against networks, systems, or applications. By carefully examining the tactics and methods used by actual cyber attackers, this investigation seeks to provide a dynamic picture of an organization's vulnerability to possible intrusions.

Objective Vulnerability Identification: Revealing the Weakness Shadows: Finding vulnerabilities objectively is the main purpose of penetration testing. Ethical hackers uncover potential points of vulnerability in digital infrastructure that could be exploited by hostile actors by closely examining every aspect of it.

This enlightening procedure acts as a lighthouse, directing businesses toward strengthening their security against possible cyberattacks.

Multiple Approaches: White-Box, Black-Box, and Gray-Box Examination: A wide range of approaches are included in penetration testing, and each one provides a distinct viewpoint on security resilience.

- **White-Box Testing:** With this method, security experts have complete access to the internal workings of the systems under test. It provides insights on weaknesses that could be obvious to someone with insider knowledge by simulating an insider's perspective.

- **Black-Box Testing:** Black-box testing simulates the viewpoint of an external attacker while operating with little to no prior knowledge. Without requiring any inside insights, this methodology evaluates the capacity to locate and take advantage of weaknesses.

- **Gray-Box Testing:** This method, which incorporates partial knowledge of the internal environment, strikes a balance between the two extremes. With this method, an attacker with little knowledge of the organization's systems is simulated.

Strategic Decision Informant: Providing Light on the Digital Environment: Organizations use the findings of penetration testing as a compass to help them make strategic decisions that strengthen their cybersecurity defenses. These well-informed choices include setting cleanup priorities and distributing resources wisely for improved protection. Penetration testing sheds light on complex cyber environments, enabling organizations to make informed decisions.

Adaptive Defense and Continuous Improvement: Changing in the Face of Threats: Penetration testing is a continuous process that depends on adaptive defense and ongoing improvement. Security strategy is always evolving, driven by the lessons learned from each testing iteration. Organizations may strengthen and adjust their defenses against the constantly changing strategies employed by cyber adversaries by accepting the lessons learnt.

2.8.9. Patch: The Essential Rhythm of Software and System Strengthening

In the complex world of software and system maintenance, a patch is the lifeblood of defense. It is a software update that has been painstakingly created by vendors to fix problems, patch security flaws, or add new features. The timely application of updates is crucial in the ever-evolving digital ecosystem as it maintains a secure environment by swiftly addressing known vulnerabilities and reducing the likelihood of cyber attackers exploiting them.

Patches' Changing Role as Defenders of Software Integrity: The dynamic role of patches as defenders of software integrity is noteworthy. They are the doctors of the digital age, identifying and treating illnesses inside complex apps and system code. Patches are proactive steps to maintain the best possible health of digital entities; they can be used to resolve security flaws that could provide entry points for cyber adversaries or to correct errors that impair performance.

Important for Security Upkeep: Reducing Hazards with Prompt Updates: Patching in a timely manner is essential for maintaining security throughout the digital ecosystem. Patching quickly becomes a strategic defense as cyber adversaries continue to try to exploit vulnerabilities. Organizations may lower their window of exposure and strengthen their digital fortifications against the ever-evolving cyber hazards by staying ahead of prospective threats.

A Strategic Ballet of Assessment and Deployment for Effective Patch Management: Patch management that works requires a calculated dance between deployment and assessment. The process commences with a thorough evaluation of vulnerabilities, pinpointing any areas of weakness that need to be addressed. Setting priorities becomes an essential step in ensuring that the most important patches—those that address serious vulnerabilities—are applied first. The next step is the methodical patch rollout, which is planned to reduce the exposure window and strengthen the digital environment against any attacks.

Reducing the Exposure Window: Accurate Patch Deployment: Reducing the time that an application is exposed to possible dangers is the fundamental goal of patch management. Organizations can shorten the time that cyber adversaries can exploit vulnerabilities by applying updates methodically and quickly. The accuracy with which patches are deployed acts as a preventative measure, making digital entities resistant to the ever-changing strategies employed by malevolent actors.

Staying Alert and Adjusting: Changing with the Digital Environment: The dynamic nature of the digital threat landscape necessitates constant vigilance and adaptability. Patch management that is effective encompasses the concepts of continuous assessment, prioritization, and deployment in addition to one-time work. Organizations can maintain the strength, resilience, and efficacy of their patch management techniques in protecting against new cyber threats by adjusting to the always changing digital landscape.

2.8.10. Social Engineering: Exposing the Complexities of Psychological Abuse

In the secretive field of cybersecurity, social engineering is a deceitful tactic used by cybercriminals to take advantage of psychological weaknesses in people. This clandestine activity involves a variety of strategies, such as baiting, pretexting, phishing, and quid pro quo. Attackers seek to set up situations in which people mistakenly reveal sensitive information, carry out illegal activities, or undermine security itself by skillfully using deceit, persuasion, or force.

Deception as a Craft: Strategies in the Social Engineering Toolbox: Social engineering is fundamentally the art of deceit. Cybercriminals are adept at using techniques like phishing, in which people are tricked into divulging personal information by emails that appear authentic. While baiting takes advantage of people's curiosity by luring them in with something appealing, pre-texting entails fabricating a scenario in order to obtain information. The trade of information for favors is known as quid pro quo, and it opens up a subtle but effective channel for abuse.

Human-Centric Threats: Taking Advantage of the Security Weakest Link: The human factor is acknowledged by social engineering as the weakest link in the security system. Attackers target human psychology in order to breach digital fortifications by persuading people rather than using technological flaws. Social engineering techniques take advantage of the natural human impulses that might unintentionally undermine security, such as the appearance of trust in phishing emails or the attraction of curiosity in baiting situations.

Meeting the Art of Deceit: Establishing a Security-Aware Culture: The establishment of a robust security awareness culture is the first line of defense against social engineering. This entails teaching people about the strategies used by cybercriminals, encouraging a critical mindset to scrutinize unexpected communications, and creating a sense of accountability in protecting confidential data. The more people are informed on social engineering techniques, the more capable they are of fending off these cunning schemes.

Continuous Education: Protecting Yourself From Psychological Trickery: The dynamics of human behavior and communication shape social engineering. As a result, continuing education is necessary to combat this art of deception. Frequent awareness campaigns, training sessions, and role-playing social engineering scenarios enable people to identify, fend off, and report any risks. Organizations build a strong defense against the constantly changing social engineering strategies by investing in ongoing education.

Putting Security Controls in Place: Technology-Based Defenses Against Threats Focused on Humans: The implementation of technical safeguards is a complementary measure to human awareness as a means of defense. Advanced email filtering, multi-factor authentication, and intrusion detection systems are examples of security mechanisms that operate as watchful guardians against attempts at social engineering. Organizations can strengthen their defenses and add more layers of protection against threats that are focused on humans by including these controls into their cybersecurity architecture.

2.8.11. Digital Perimeter Sentinel: The Intrusion Detection System (IDS)

As the watchful guardian of the digital domain, an intrusion detection system (IDS) is responsible for keeping an eye on network or system activity for any indications of unusual activity, policy infractions, or any security risks. This digital watchdog uses a variety of detection techniques, such as heuristic analysis, anomaly detection, and signature-based detection, to keep a close eye on the complex world of digital activity. The intrusion detection system (IDS) takes proactive measures to strengthen the digital perimeter by issuing alerts or initiating pre-planned corrective actions when it detects suspicious activity.

The Vigilant Eye of IDS: Protecting Digital Domains: An IDS is essentially the vigilant eye that guards digital spaces. It constantly monitors the operations of the system or network, watching closely for any departures from accepted practices or signs of possible security risks. In order to detect and reduce hazards before they become serious breaches, proactive surveillance is necessary.

Multiple Detection Techniques: Creating a Harmony of Alertness: An IDS's effectiveness is derived from its variety of detection techniques, each of which adds to the overall chorus of alertness.

- **Signature-Based Detection:** In this technique, established attack patterns or signatures are compared with observed activity. The action is flagged by the IDS as potentially dangerous if a match is discovered.

- **Anomaly Detection:** This technique finds deviations from the norm that might point to odd or malevolent activity by setting up a baseline of typical behavior.

- **Heuristic Analysis:** This technique examines patterns and behaviors that might not correspond to recognized signatures but yet show signs of possible dangers. The detection procedure gains flexibility from heuristic analysis.

Avoidive Warning Production and Remedial Measures: Strengthening the Digital

Barrier: An IDS is not just a passive spectator when it finds suspicious activity; it actively helps to strengthen the digital perimeter. Cybersecurity teams are alerted to possible risks by the system. To provide a prompt and focused response to any intrusions, IDS can also be set up to perform predetermined corrective actions, including banning particular IP addresses or isolating affected systems.

A Collective Defense: Contributing to the Overall Cybersecurity Posture: An IDS is an essential part that enhances the overall cybersecurity posture; it is not a stand-alone device. It acts as a front-line defense mechanism, bolstering existing security measures in the ongoing endeavor to build a resilient digital environment by continually monitoring and reacting to possible incursions.

Ongoing Development: Adjusting to New Dangers: An intrusion detection system's efficacy depends on its capacity to adapt to new threats as they arise. Consistent updates to detection signatures, optimization of anomaly detection algorithms, and integration of heuristic analysis improvements guarantee that the intrusion detection system (IDS) stays a resilient and flexible protector against the constantly changing strategies employed by cybercriminals.

2.8.12. The Vital Foundation of Device Fortification: Endpoint Security

One important subfield of the larger field of cybersecurity is called endpoint security, and it is the cornerstone concerned with protecting end-user devices, or endpoints. These gadgets, which include mobile phones and laptops as well as PCs, serve as the front lines through which users engage with the digital environment. The technologies that comprise advanced endpoint security solutions include intrusion prevention systems, device management tools, and antivirus software. This powerful combination of defenses has one main function: it protects individual devices from ransomware, malware, and phishing attempts, among other cyberthreats.

The Changing Endpoint Environment: PCs, Laptops, and Mobile Devices: Fundamentally, endpoint security acknowledges the ever-changing endpoint landscape. These include a variety of gadgets, each of which could serve as a point of entry for online dangers. Users connect and engage with the digital world through computers, laptops, and mobile devices, which create the nexus. In order to provide a robust defense against the various and complex attacks that are common in the interconnected digital ecosystem, it becomes imperative to secure these endpoints.

All-Inclusive Technologies: The Endpoint Security Weaponry: Endpoint security is a suite of complete technologies that are deliberately deployed to fortify devices, rather than a single solution.

- **Antivirus Software:** This reliable guardian detects and removes harmful software, keeping endpoints safe from malware intrusion.

- **Intrusion Prevention Systems:** These systems serve as watchful gatekeepers, proactively detecting and blocking possible intrusions before they jeopardize the integrity of endpoints.

- **Device Management technologies:** These technologies give businesses fine-grained control over how endpoints are configured, guaranteeing compliance with security guidelines and facilitating quick fixes for any vulnerabilities.

A Stronger Digital Periphery for Defense Against Various Cyberthreats: Endpoint security is equipped with a variety of technologies that work together to protect against various cyber threats. Endpoint security acts as a rock solid barrier between users and the potential harm that lurks in the digital shadows, protecting them from everything from the sneaky infiltration attempts of malware to the coercive methods of ransomware and the deceitful maneuvers of phishing assaults.

Improving the General Security Situation: A Group Defense Approach: Endpoint security is an essential part of improving an organization's overall security posture; it is not an isolated endeavor. By reinforcing individual devices, it contributes to the collective defense against weaknesses that may be exploited in the interconnected digital landscape. This collective defensive strategy is vital in the face of the ever-evolving techniques utilized by cyber enemies.

Digital Terrain Navigation: Information as the Guide: Understanding the subtleties of endpoint security gives individuals with a profound understanding and insight essential to traverse the complicated and ever-evolving landscape of cybersecurity. Understanding endpoint security concepts is essential for developing complete cybersecurity strategies in the connected world because endpoints act as consumers' primary digital interfaces.

Understanding endpoint security ideas is a key to navigating the ever-changing world of digital fortification, both for individuals and companies, in the complex field of cybersecurity. The fundamental knowledge of endpoint security strengthens the digital perimeters against the many and complex dangers that are common in the digital sphere, acting as more than just a device shield as cyber threats change.

CHAPTER THREE

3.0 Opening Up the Ethical Hacking Universe

Explore the nuances of ethical hacking, a crucial field of cybersecurity that crosses conventional boundaries. We peel back the many layers of ethical hacking in this chapter, giving you a thorough grasp of its tenets, practices, and moral implications.

3.1. Ethical Hacking Definition: Understanding the Digital Guardians

Take a trip down memory lane with us as we explore the fundamentals of ethical hacking. Fundamentally, ethical hacking is the forefront of digital stewardship, where knowledgeable individuals use their knowledge to strengthen the digital domain against potentially harmful attacks.

The Goal
Instead of being a covert operation, ethical hacking is a calculated, legal tactic used to

identify weaknesses before malevolent actors take advantage of them. It is a proactive strategy that recognizes that maintaining security is an ongoing effort that calls for awareness and caution.

Responsible Guardians

Equipped with express consent, ethical hackers position themselves as protectors as opposed to invaders. They make sure their actions are in line with the fundamentals of ethical and legal cybersecurity practices by operating within the moral and legal parameters established by organizations.

Systems, Networks, and Applications Safety

The scope of ethical hacking includes networks, systems, and applications. These digital stewards carefully evaluate and examine the complex architecture of these organizations, looking for weak points and potential openings that could be used by adversaries.

Reducing Possible Malevolent Risks

Preemptively identifying and addressing vulnerabilities is the main goal of ethical hacking in order to reduce the likelihood of prospective hostile threats. Through the adoption of an adversarial mindset, ethical hackers proactively fortify digital defenses, guaranteeing resilience against constantly changing cyber threats.

Defensive Strategy Position

Ethical hacking is a proactive protective stance rather than just a reaction to online dangers. It entails taking a rigorous and systematic approach to finding flaws, enabling organizations to fix vulnerabilities before they become exploitable and preserve the integrity of their digital infrastructure.

Regarding ethical hacking, comprehending its fundamental goal, the moral limits it upholds, and its tactical function in defending digital environments opens the door to a thorough comprehension of the crucial role these virtual sentinels play in strengthening our globalized society.

3.2 Tools for Digital Defense: The Ethical Hacker's Toolbox

Take a tour through the advanced toolkit that ethical hackers utilize to expose the tactical weapons they use in the ongoing struggle for cyber defense.

Accuracy of Penetration Testing

Penetration testing, which is the rigorous modeling of intrusions to uncover weaknesses, is at the forefront of an ethical hacker's toolbox. Ethical hackers expertly maneuver through systems, imitating possible enemies to reveal vulnerabilities and reinforce virtual fortifications against unapproved entry.

Evaluations of Vulnerability

Vulnerability assessments are used by ethical hackers to thoroughly examine systems and networks. They identify possible weak areas by carefully inspecting them, determining the level of vulnerability, and giving businesses a plan for strategic rehabilitation.

Tools and Methods for Cutting-Edge

Modern methods and tools abound in the ethical hacker's arsenal. These tools, which range from network scanners and intrusion detection systems to complex attack frameworks, enable ethical hackers to explore the digital landscape in great detail and make sure that no vulnerability eludes their careful inspection.

Strategic Awareness

For ethical hackers, scouting is a tactical skill. They use cutting-edge tools to collect data on networks, systems, and applications, giving them a comprehensive understanding of the digital environment. The defensive tactics employed by ethical hackers are built upon this reconnaissance.

Adaptive and Flexible Methods

Since cyber dangers are always changing, ethical hackers modify their strategies on the go. They make sure their toolkit stays at the vanguard of digital defense, prepared to tackle the constantly evolving tactics of prospective attackers, by keeping up with innovative tools and strategies.

Preventive Defense

The ethical hacker's toolbox is a representation of proactive protection rather than just a set of tools. Ethical hackers strengthen firms against potential cyber risks by carefully using these tools, guaranteeing a safe and secure digital environment.

By delving into an ethical hacker's toolkit, one can uncover the intricacy and accuracy of digital defense and comprehend how these professionals use technology to protect the integrity of our globalized society.

3.3 Practical Applications of Ethical Hacking

Enter the domain where ethical hacking goes from theory to practical application. Examine concrete instances that show how ethical hackers actively strengthen cybersecurity protections in actual situations, permanently altering the resilience of digital ecosystems.

Scenario 1: Accuracy of Penetration Testing: To do a penetration test on its vital infrastructure, a company hires ethical hackers. By painstakingly simulating a targeted cyberattack, ethical hackers find weaknesses that malevolent actors might exploit. The organization strengthens its systems against possible breaches by means of this proactive testing.

Scenario 2: Exercises with Red and Blue Teams: In simulated combat, ethical hackers take on opposing teams in which the "Red Team" aims to compromise defenses while the "Blue Team" resists these assaults. Through this cooperative effort, companies are able to evaluate their readiness, pinpoint areas of vulnerability, and improve their defensive tactics by taking into account actual hostile strategies.

Scenario 3: Bug Bounty Initiatives: Businesses start bug bounty programs to encourage ethical hackers everywhere to find and report security holes in their systems. Motivated by prizes and recognition, ethical hackers voluntarily contribute by revealing vulnerabilities that are concealed, allowing organizations to repair them before bad actors may take advantage of them.

Scenario 4: Simulations of Incident Response: In order to evaluate an organization's capacity for detection, reaction, and recovery, ethical hackers plan and carry out incident response simulations that resemble cyberattacks. These practical exercises support ongoing development and offer priceless insights into how well an organization's incident response procedures work.

Scenario 5: Evaluations of Application Security: Ethical hackers concentrate on closely examining online application security to find any vulnerabilities that can result in data breaches. Through the discovery of security flaws like SQL injections and cross-site scripting, ethical hackers enable companies to put strong security measures in place and safeguard confidential information.

Impact on the Resilience of Cybersecurity: These practical uses for ethical hacking highlight how important it is to improving cybersecurity resilience. Ethical hackers actively participate in the ongoing fight against cyber threats by finding and fixing vulnerabilities and improving incident response protocols, ensuring that the digital environment is safe and flexible.

By exploring these possibilities, one comes to understand the genuine value of ethical hacking in strengthening the digital sphere against ever changing cyber threats.

3.4. Handling Ethical Conundrums: Cybersecurity's Balancing Act

Explore the moral conundrums that arise in the field of ethical hacking, where cyber-guardians must strike a careful balance between bolstering defenses and respecting the concepts of privacy and secrecy. This section explores the complexities of ethical issues, emphasizing the significance of morally righteous behavior.

The Careful Equilibrium: Strictly testing digital defenses to find weaknesses, ethical hackers maintain a delicate balance. This procedure presents moral conundrums, especially in regards to how far these experts should examine systems without breaching confidentiality or invading personal privacy.

Privacy Issues: Sensitive information may come into contact with ethical hackers while they search for flaws. Ensuring that personal information is treated with the highest care and that privacy rights are respected is an ethical challenge. A crucial component of ethical hacking techniques is finding a balance between efficient testing and protecting user privacy.

Difficulties with Confidentiality: Confidential material is frequently accessed by ethical hackers while doing evaluations. Setting limits on how this information is handled is necessary to navigate the ethical terrain and make sure it is neither revealed nor abused. Frameworks for ethical hacking place a strong emphasis on the necessity of upholding confidentiality even in the face of potentially damaging discoveries.

Ethical Frameworks and Guidelines: In order to solve these problems, ethical hacking follows pre-established rules and conventions. Professional associations like EC-Council and ISACA have established industry-standard codes of conduct that establish ethical guidelines for practitioners. These frameworks highlight responsible disclosure, informed consent, and transparency as the cornerstones of ethical hacking.

Courtesy and Legal Method: Exploration with no boundaries is not permitted while using ethical hacking. Professionals in this domain stay within ethical and legal bounds, making sure that everything they do complies with national and international regulations. The integrity of cybersecurity procedures and the preservation of public trust are greatly impacted by ethical hacking done responsibly.

Ongoing Self-Reflection and Adjustment: The ethical conundrums around hacking change along with technology. Ethical hackers reflect on a constant basis and modify their methods to conform to new ethical standards. This innovative strategy makes sure that ethical hacking upholds individual rights and continues to improve cybersecurity.

Ethical hackers contribute to a cybersecurity environment that promotes digital security and ethical values by skillfully navigating these ethical problems.

3.5. Ethical Hacking Continuous Learning: Staying One Step Ahead

Set out on a quest to comprehend the ever-changing landscape of ethical hacking and the critical role that ongoing education plays in remaining one step ahead. To stay ahead of the curve in the quickly changing world of ethical hacking methods and cybersecurity risks, professionals need to take preventative measures.

Switching to Counter New Dangers: In ethical hacking, one must always be on the lookout for new cybersecurity dangers. Ethical hackers need to keep up with the most recent attack vectors, vulnerabilities, and exploit techniques as malevolent techniques change. With this expertise, they are equipped with the understanding necessary to effectively predict and fight evolving threats.

Examining Sophisticated Instruments and Methods: The discipline of ethical hacking is known for its inventiveness; new methods and instruments are frequently introduced. By exploring and mastering cutting-edge techniques, ethical hackers can improve their proficiency in vulnerability assessment, penetration testing, and overall digital protection through continuous learning. By doing this investigation, ethical hackers can be confident that they are prepared to handle complex cyberattacks.

Partnering with the Community of Ethical Hackers: Engagement in the ethical hacking community is a crucial component of lifelong learning. Collaborative platforms, conferences, and forums offer professional spaces for exchanging ideas, talking about new developments, and learning from one another's experiences. Interacting with the community promotes a team approach to being knowledgeable and adjusting to the changing threat environment.

Practice in-hand and through simulation: Practical knowledge is essential for ethical hacking, and ongoing education frequently calls for practical experience. Capture the flag (CTF) exercises, realistic scenarios, and simulated settings all aid in the development of skills and readiness. Problem-solving abilities, critical thinking, and the capacity to apply academic knowledge in practical contexts are all improved by practical experience.

Accreditations and Instructional Plans: Specialized training programs and certifications provide reinforcement for ongoing education. Certifications in ethical hacking, like the Offensive Security Certified Professional (OSCP) or Certified Ethical Hacker (CEH), verify knowledge and need to be renewed on an ongoing basis. Through these training, ethical hackers are guaranteed to stay current on industry standards and best practices.

Professional Conduct and Ethics: In ethical hacking, ongoing education covers ethical issues and professional behavior in addition to technical skills. Ethical hackers keep up with modifications to laws pertaining to privacy, ethics, and regulations. In the cybersecurity sector, upholding integrity and trust requires a dedication to moral behavior.

Career Development Strategy: In the dynamic field of ethical hacking, ongoing education is a calculated strategy to professional growth. Individuals in the cybersecurity industry that place a high value on continuing education show that they are dedicated to excellence and flexibility.

Through a commitment to lifelong learning, ethical hackers improve not only their own skills but also the overall robustness of digital systems. Ethical hacking can continue to be a proactive and effective means of thwarting cyberattacks by staying one step ahead of the game.

3.6. In Beyond of Technical Expertise: The Human Factor in Ethical Hacking

Acknowledge the significant influence of the human factor in ethical hacking, which goes beyond technological expertise. In this investigation, we examine the critical roles that good communication, soft skills, and an ethical attitude play in the success of ethical hackers.

Soft Skills for Hacking Ethically: Technical proficiency is essential, but ethical hackers also need to possess strong soft skills. The capacity to communicate, solve problems, think critically, and be flexible are crucial for overcoming the challenges presented by ethical hacking. These abilities allow ethical hackers to work well in interdisciplinary teams, comprehend user viewpoints, and clearly communicate security problems.

Interaction and Cooperation: It is rare for ethical hacking to be a solo endeavor. When ethical hackers collaborate with developers, stakeholders, and other cybersecurity experts, effective communication and teamwork are essential. It guarantees that security insights are properly understood when results, threats, and mitigation methods are well articulated, which promotes a proactive and cooperative security culture.

Ethical Perspective and Openness: The foundation of responsible hacking activities is an ethical mentality. Ethical hackers are required to follow a strict code of ethics that places a premium on confidentiality, privacy, and legal compliance. It is imperative to report vulnerabilities and potential dangers in a transparent manner. By doing this, companies can respond to problems quickly and build a trustworthy relationship between ethical hackers and the targets they are trying to safeguard.

Client-First Perspective: Taking a user-centric approach is necessary to comprehend the human element. Understanding how users interact with systems and applications is essential for ethical hackers to foresee potential weaknesses brought on by user behavior. The ability of an ethical hacker to recognize and successfully address security flaws is improved by this sympathetic awareness.

Successful Documentation and Reporting: The significance of ethical hacking rests not only in finding vulnerabilities but also in effectively communicating discoveries. The ability to write thorough and comprehensible reports is a prerequisite for ethical hackers. Organizations can use this paper as a useful tool to prioritize and put the required security measures in place.

Everlasting Professional Growth: Soft skills need to be continuously developed because they are dynamic. Committed to their own and their careers' development, ethical hackers actively participate in workshops, training programs, and educational opportunities that improve their interpersonal, communication, and teamwork abilities. This dedication enhances the overall impact and efficacy of ethical hacking initiatives.

Building a Culture of Ethics: Ethical hacking is a cultural perspective as much as a technological technique. The development of an ethical culture in companies is greatly aided by ethical hackers. Ethical hackers contribute to a culture where security is a shared responsibility by modeling ethical behavior, encouraging transparency, and encouraging teamwork.

By accepting the human component, ethical hackers advance their field beyond technical expertise and become essential players in the larger cybersecurity scene. Ethical hackers ensure a comprehensive and robust strategy to digital protection by bridging the gap between technology and human understanding through effective communication, ethical mindsets, and collaborative efforts.

3.7. Prospective Views: Ethical Hacking in the Cybersecurity Environment of Tomorrow

Set out on a quest to investigate the potential applications of ethical hacking and its crucial role in influencing the cybersecurity environment of the future. In order to protect digital ecosystems, ethical hacking continues to be at the forefront as technology develops and new threats appear.

Evolving Technologies and Hacking Ethics: Emerging technologies are interwoven with ethical hacking in the future. The intricacies of blockchain technology, artificial intelligence, machine learning, and the Internet of Things (IoT) are all easily navigated by ethical hackers. By comprehending the ways in which these technologies affect cybersecurity, ethical hackers are able to foresee weaknesses and create strong defenses.

Adjusting to Changing Dangers: Cyber dangers are always changing, bringing with them fresh difficulties and ways to attack. Future ethical hackers will have to adjust to new threats including ransomware, sophisticated social engineering techniques, and attacks based on quantum computing. Being proactive and anticipatory is necessary to stay ahead of dangerous actors.

Ethical Hacking Integrated Into DevSecOps: Ethical hacking will be smoothly incorporated into DevSecOps procedures in the future. The importance of cooperation between development teams and ethical hackers increases as security becomes a critical component of the software development life cycle. DevSecOps's shift guarantees that security is given top priority from the beginning of every digital project.

International Cooperation and Threat Information: Ethical hackers will use threat intelligence and collaborate globally more and more. The combined efforts of ethical hacking communities become crucial as cyber dangers become more international. Global exchange of threat intelligence, best practices, and insights strengthens the group's defenses against cyberattacks.

Recent Developments in Law and Regulation: There will be improvements in legal frameworks and legislation pertaining to ethical hacking in the future. There will be an increase in standardized procedures and clear norms, which will give ethical hackers a better defined working environment. Governments and institutions around the world will come to understand how important ethical hackers are to improving cybersecurity.

Expertise in Ethical Hacking: There will be an increase in the prominence of ethical hacking specializations. Niche markets like cloud security, industrial control systems, or Internet of Things security may be of interest to ethical hackers. By specializing, ethical hackers can become experts in particular fields and offer focused and efficient security solutions.

Programs for Education and Skill Development:
Initiatives in the field of education will be crucial to meeting future demands. Academic curricula and training programs will change to incorporate the newest methods, instruments, and technologies. The emphasis will be on ongoing skill improvement to make sure ethical hackers are prepared to take on new challenges.

A Preemptive Approach to Defense:
Ethical hacking will be acknowledged in the future as both a proactive and reactive defensive tactic. Businesses will spend more money on ethical hacking services in order to find vulnerabilities and fix them before bad actors can take advantage of them. This change makes the cybersecurity posture more robust.

Looking ahead, ethical hacking is going to be a vital and ever-changing part of cybersecurity. Because of their versatility, skill, and dedication to moral values, ethical hackers will always be the stewards of our digital future, making sure that cyberspace is safe and stable for future generations.

3.8 Foundations of Computer Hacking: Dissecting the Digital Intricacies

Learning the fundamentals of computer hacking is a crucial endeavor in the dynamic and always changing field of cybersecurity. This investigation not only sheds light on the tactics used by both bad actors and ethical hackers, but it also offers a fundamental manual for strengthening digital defenses against possible intrusions. Let's take a thorough tour and dissect the essential elements that make up the complex field of computer hacking.

3.8.1. Computer Hacking Definition: Getting Around the Challenging Landscape

Comprehending the Complex World of Cyberattacks

The phrase "computer hacking" is a broad one that refers to a variety of actions that involve the illegal access, alteration, or use of computer systems, networks, or data. It is a symbol of a complex dance between digital invaders and the technological fortresses that goes beyond the bounds of traditional usage. Computer hacking is essentially the act of persistently trying to get past security measures, get unauthorized access to systems, and carry out actions with the intention of accessing data without authorization, disrupting systems, or achieving other evil goals.

A Symphony of Intrusion: The Tapestry of Techniques

The dance between the attacker and the defense is arranged by a symphony of tactics in the vast field of computer hacking. These methods include both the deft manipulation of code and the purposeful evasion of security standards, as well as the subtle exploitation of weaknesses. Like a concerto in digital form, the hacker uses these strategies deftly to move through the complex world of ones and zeros in search of openings to take advantage of.

Moral Crossroads: Ethical vs. Malevolent Hacking

It is crucial to negotiate the ethical juncture that the term of computer hacking presents. One route involves ethical hacking, a commendable endeavor carried out with express consent to enhance security. White-hat hackers, or ethical hackers, work with corporations to find and fix security holes, strengthening digital integrity as a whole in the process. The other route is occupied by malevolent hacking, an esoteric activity that directly jeopardizes digital security. The black-hat equivalents of malicious hackers, or "bad hackers," use unapproved exploits for malicious, disruptive, or selfish purposes.

Disclosing Intentions: From Unauthorized Entry to Disruption of the System

Computer hacking has a variety of motivations, ranging from the covert goal of gaining unauthorized access to the more overt goal of disrupting the system. Malicious actors could break into systems to steal confidential data, tamper with data integrity, or take advantage of weaknesses for their own benefit. The goals that drive hacking activities—whether they be monetary gains, political objectives, or sheer hate—influence how these cyberattacks unfold.

**Thoughts for Digital Defenders: Crossing
the Thin Line**

The definition of computer hacking reveals that
there is a range along which this digital
phenomenon operates. Cybersecurity
professionals and digital defenders might gain
important insights from comprehending the
many layers of hacking. It acts as a compass,
directing organizations on how to strengthen
their protections against manipulation,
exploitation, and unapproved access. Because
the field of cybersecurity is always changing, it
becomes crucial to walk this fine line between
ethical and malevolent hacking.

3.8.2. Common Hacking Methods: Understanding Cyber Adversaries' Strategies

The Changing Domain of Hacking Methods: A
Multifaceted Scene: The world of hacking is a
dynamic environment that is defined by the
wide range of tactics that cyber adversaries
utilize. Every method has unique properties of
its own, a digital signature that indicates how it
operates inside the complex web of hacking
activities.

Social Engineering: The Craft of Trickery and Manipulation

Social Engineering is proof positive of hackers' psychological skills. Through psychological tricks or other misleading tactics, people are tricked into becoming unsuspecting pawns in this approach, which causes them to expose critical information. Because it is based on human psychology, this type of exploitation gives opponents a subtle but effective tool.

Phishing: Illusory Plans Revealed:

Phishing is the artful dance of deception masterminded by hackers. Users can be fooled into disclosing private information using emails, messages, or phony websites. The attractiveness of communication that appears to be authentic conceals the hidden goal of obtaining private information, emphasizing the devious tactics used by enemies.

Malware: The Cunning Encroacher

The sneaky intruder *Malware* appears in the hacker's toolbox. This category includes a wide range of malicious software intended to steal data, compromise systems, or interfere with regular computer operations. Malware, which can range from viruses to ransomware, is a flexible tool used by enemies with a variety of goals.

Aggressive Assaults: The Strength of Durability

Brute Force Attacks demonstrate the tremendous amount of computing power that opponents can muster. With this technique, password tries are made repeatedly until the right one is found. Brute force attacks exist because they are predicated on the idea that an attacker's superior computing power would eventually crack even the most complicated passwords.

SQL Injection: Utilizing Vulnerabilities in Databases

SQL Injection explores the weaknesses present in database queries. These flaws are used by adversaries to obtain unauthorized access to private data kept in databases. This method emphasizes how crucial database structure security is in preventing possible intrusions.

Injecting Malicious Code using Cross-Site Scripting (XSS)

Cross-Site Scripting (XSS) elevates hacking methods to a new level of complexity.

Adversaries might lead users to malicious websites or compromise user data by inserting malicious JavaScript into websites. This method draws attention to the code injection vulnerability of web applications, highlighting the importance of strong security protocols in the digital domain.

Traversing the Digital Terrain: Defenders' Alertness:

For defenders navigating the constantly changing digital terrain, it becomes imperative that they comprehend these typical hacking strategies. Every method signifies a possible avenue of attack that establishments need to protect themselves from. Defenders need to be alert and take proactive steps to protect themselves from the many and complex hacking techniques used by adversaries who are constantly evolving their tactics.

3.8.3. Hacking Motivations: Exposing the Varied Goals

Multiple Drives: A Tapestry of Goals: The reasons for hacking activities are a complex and varied tapestry, with each thread contributing to a distinct story that outlines the goals of cyber attackers. In this ever-changing environment, reasons for hacking could vary from the desire for monetary gain to activism, cyberwarfare, strategic espionage, and even the challenge that hacking poses for oneself.

Money Gain: The Seduction of Unlawful Wealth:

Financial Gain is a powerful motivator that propels hacking activities. Adversaries use dishonest means to obtain financial gain, such as stealing confidential financial data, committing fraud, or taking advantage of holes in financial systems. The temptation of money obtained through illegal means becomes a powerful motivator for many hacking operations.

Security: Pursuing a Gainful Advantage:

Espionage manifests as a strategic incentive, frequently linked to actions supported by governments or corporations. Adversaries use hacking to obtain private data with the intention of outwitting rivals in the political, technological, or economic spheres. Because espionage is inherently covert, hackers are motivated to penetrate digital barriers in order to obtain confidential information.

Activism: Ideological Cause Hacking

Hacking actions that support political, social, or ideological reasons are motivated by *activism*. Adversaries use their digital skills to advance their own goals, such as upending social conventions or fostering social change. Hacking turns into a tool for activism, giving people or organizations a digital platform to spread their message.

Cyberwarfare: The Digital Front Line of National Security

Cyber Warfare refers to hacking actions carried out as a component of nation-state conflicts, transcending personal objectives. In order to obtain a tactical edge, enemies in this field try to interfere with or breach digital infrastructure. The digital battlefield turns into a stage for clandestine fights between states showcasing their technological capabilities.

Individual Task: The Excitement of Technical Mastery:

Some hackers are driven not only by financial gain but also by the "Personal Challenge" that hacking offers. Hacking becomes a way to test one's technological skills, escape from reality, or satisfy an intellectual curiosity. This particular group of hackers aims to push their abilities to the limit by delving into digital systems for the pure pleasure of learning and becoming experts.

Recognizing Motives: The Defenders' Imperative

It becomes essential for cybersecurity defenders to comprehend the reasons behind hacking. It offers perceptions into opponents' motivations, directing the creation of strong defense plans. Defendants can build a strong defense against the complex array of cyberthreats by identifying the various goals that spur hacking activity and adjusting their reaction accordingly.

3.8.4. Cybersecurity Countermeasures: Creating Robust Barriers

Digital Citadel Protection: An All-encompassing Strategy: Strong cybersecurity measures must be put in place to protect against the constant threat of hacking. To strengthen the digital barriers and foil any breaches, defenders employ a diverse range of technologies and tactics in this ever-changing environment.

Firewalls: The Watchmen on the Network

Firewalls appear as sturdy protectors, set up to keep an eye on and regulate network traffic. By acting as virtual gatekeepers and thwarting illegal access, these network security solutions strengthen the digital border. Firewalls provide a solid barrier against possible incursions by enforcing predetermined security rules, providing a baseline defense against hacking attempts.

Antivirus Software: Guard Your System Against Malevolent Intrusions

As a watchful sentinel, Antivirus Software finds and eliminates harmful software that jeopardizes digital integrity. Antivirus programs serve as an essential first line of defense against a variety of malware threats, including viruses and ransomware. They prevent systems and networks from falling victim to the stealthy scope of hacking campaigns by detecting and eliminating harmful code.

Encryption: Digital Secrets Encoded for Protection

In the cybersecurity playbook, encryption is the main player, applying methods to safeguard data through encoding. This tactical move guards against unwanted access and guarantees the privacy of important data. Encryption is a strong protection against hacking because it converts data into ciphertext, which makes it unintelligible to malevolent organizations trying to access it without authorization.

Fixes as Barriers Against Vulnerabilities: Regular Updates

A proactive method to fix known vulnerabilities and improve the overall security posture is the release of *Regular Updates*. Defenders build a dynamic defense mechanism that adjusts to the changing threat landscape by applying patches and updates. This tactical strategy makes sure that systems are protected from various attack vectors, which reduces the chance of exploitation.

Empowering the Human Firewall with Security Awareness Training

Security Awareness Training is essential to developing an organization's proactive security culture. Users who receive education are better equipped to identify and steer clear of such hazards, which makes them a formidable barrier against hacking attempts. Organizations can strengthen their human firewall and fortify it against adversaries' strategies, such as social engineering, by cultivating a heightened awareness of security.

Integrating Measures: A Comprehensive Guard Against Cyberattacks:

The combination of these cybersecurity techniques forges a strong barrier against hackers and a comprehensive shield for digital assets and systems. Implementing thorough cybersecurity safeguards becomes essential as technology advances and hacking techniques get more complex. In order to outmaneuver the ever-changing world of cyber attacks, defenders must adopt a proactive approach and continuously refine and adjust their techniques.

3.8.5. Deciphering the Legal Repercussions of Unauthorized Hacking

Examining the Legal Environment: A Grave Offense:

Participating in unapproved hacking operations carries a risk of serious legal repercussions. Hacking is classified as a criminal offense by laws and regulations worldwide, which means that anyone who engages in it may face prosecution, heavy fines, and even jail time. The legal ramifications of unapproved hacking activities create a strong framework that discourages and punishes people who try to penetrate digital barriers without authorization.

Hacking Is Now Recognized as a Crime Worldwide

Every legal system in the world acknowledges hacking as a grave offense. Laws specifically prohibiting the unlawful use, alteration, or exploitation of computer systems, networks, or data have been passed in several nations. These legislative frameworks demonstrate a shared commitment to protecting digital integrity by establishing a collective position against destructive hacking operations.

Heavy Penalties: Legal Action, Penalties, and Prison Time

People who are discovered to have engaged in unlawful hacking may be subject to a number of harsh sanctions. Legal authorities actively pursue offenders to establish accountability, making prosecution a serious possibility. As a financial consequence, substantial fines are imposed in accordance with the seriousness of the offense. The possibility of imprisonment highlights society's intolerance for individuals who attempt to breach digital security through unapproved methods.

Legal and Responsibly Approaching Ethical Hacking

Ethical Hacking arises as a legitimate and responsible method of evaluating and fortifying cybersecurity defenses, as opposed to unapproved hacking. Ethical hacking is the practice of expert professionals examining digital systems to find flaws with express permission. This approved procedure enhances overall cybersecurity resilience in addition to adhering to legal requirements.

Defenders' Imperative: Cyberspace Ethics: The legal ramifications of hacking highlight the need for defenders and cybersecurity experts to act ethically in cyberspace. By creating a legitimate path for examining and strengthening digital defenses, ethical hacking enables qualified experts to add to the overall security of digital ecosystems. Defenders are essential to keeping digital landscapes intact because they uphold moral and legal standards.

3.8.6 Defensive Hacking with Ethical Hacking: Guarding Against Cyber Threats

Ethical Hacking Explained: Uncovering Penetration Testing

Ethical Hacking, often known as penetration testing, is emerging as a tactical defensive approach in the dynamic field of cybersecurity. In order to find and fix vulnerabilities in digital systems, qualified personnel simulate cyberattacks in this approved activity. As defenders of digital integrity, ethical hackers use their knowledge to examine, evaluate, and strengthen security protocols.

A Critical Role in the Proactive Identification of Weaknesses

Proactively identifying vulnerabilities in digital defenses is the core of ethical hacking. Cyberattacks are painstakingly simulated by licensed experts who examine networks, systems, and apps for weaknesses. By taking this proactive stance, ethical hackers can identify possible weak holes in systems before bad actors can take use of them.

Improving Security Resilience: A Team Approach

Beyond merely identifying vulnerabilities, ethical hackers actively work to fix them. Ethical hackers help to strengthen cybersecurity defenses continuously by working with corporations and security teams. By working together, we can make sure that vulnerabilities are not only found but also fixed, strengthening the overall security resilience of digital ecosystems.

Encouraging an Inquisitive and Flexible Position

A proactive and adaptable security posture is greatly enhanced by ethical hacking. Instead of waiting for cyberattacks to happen, companies actively recruit ethical hackers to perform regular audits. Using insights from simulated cyberattacks, defenders can constantly evolve and strengthen their defenses, staying one step ahead of adversaries.

An Ongoing Contribution to Cybersecurity: A Continuous Cycle of Improvement

The dynamic nature of cybersecurity is reflected in the ongoing cycle of improvement that ethical hacking operates within. In order to recognize and resolve emerging vulnerabilities, ethical hackers modify their tactics as technology advances and new threats materialize. This continuous support for cybersecurity guarantees that defenses continue to be strong in the face of a constantly evolving digital environment.

3.8.7. Ongoing Education in the Cybersecurity Environment:

Computer hacking is a dynamic field that requires constant study and adjustment. Organizations, ethical hackers, and cybersecurity specialists need to stay up to date on the latest defensive techniques, vulnerabilities, and threats. Maintaining awareness of developing trends and engaging in ongoing education are key components of a proactive and resilient strategy for fending against the constantly shifting terrain of digital infiltration.

Knowing the fundamentals of computer hacking is a fundamental step in delving into the complexity of cybersecurity, not just a superficial investigation. Equipped with this understanding, people and institutions can maneuver over the digital terrain with enhanced consciousness, strengthening their barriers against possible hazards and augmenting a more secure digital milieu.

3.9. Basic Security Principles: An All-Inclusive Guide to Protecting the Digital Frontier

The fundamental security principles serve as the cornerstone for protecting people, businesses, and the extensive digital ecosystems they traverse in the dynamic world of cyberspace. These guiding principles, deeply anchored in the fundamentals of cybersecurity, provide a comprehensive framework to manage risks, counteract threats, and protect the integrity of digital assets. In order to provide a strong defense against the intricacies of the digital frontier, let's take a closer look at these core ideas that form the basis of basic security.

1. The CIA Triad—confidentiality, integrity, and availability—are the cornerstones of digital defense.

Unveiling the Core Tenets: The Essence of the CIA Triad:

The CIA Triad, meaning for Confidentiality, Integrity, and Availability, emerges as the cornerstone of basic security strategy, embodying the key pillars that support digital defense. Within this trio lies the essence of securing the digital realm against varied threats and maintaining a resilient and secure information ecosystem.

Confidentiality: Shielding Sensitive Information from Prying Eyes

Confidentiality is the first pillar, encapsulating the necessity of guaranteeing that confidential data is only accessed by authorized personnel or systems. This preventive action provides a safe haven where classified information is protected from the constant risk of unwanted access by preventing digital assets from being disclosed without authorization.

Respecting the Truth in the Information Ecosystem with Integrity:

As the second pillar, *Integrity* has a central role, representing the dedication to ensure the precision and dependability of data. This fundamental idea guards against unapproved modification or tampering, maintaining the reliability of information in the digital environment. Organizations that maintain integrity foster a culture that depends on the veracity of digital data.

Availability: Facilitating Smooth and Effective Digital Journeys

The third pillar, Availability, comes into play here, guaranteeing that data and systems are consistently available to authorized users when they need them. This pillar encourages a smooth and effective digital experience by rejecting interruptions. Organizations that put availability first build a digital infrastructure that facilitates unrestricted user access to information, increasing accessibility and productivity.

Interconnected Strength: The CIA Triad's Synergy

The CIA Triad's interconnectedness is its ultimate strength. These three pillars work together to form a strong and all-encompassing security plan rather than separately. The CIA Triad serves as a framework for companies navigating the complex world of digital threats. It provides a tactical method for strengthening digital defenses and upholding the ideals of availability, secrecy, and integrity.

2. Validation and Permission:
The effectiveness of authentication and authorization procedures is closely related to the robustness of fundamental security.

- **Authentication:** Using techniques like passwords, biometrics, or multi-factor authentication to provide a secure entry point, authentication processes are enforced to verify the identity of persons or systems requesting access.

- **Authorization:** guaranteeing that users or systems can only access resources for which they have explicit permission by defining granular permissions and access controls in line with assigned roles and responsibilities.

3. Intrusion Detection Systems (IDS) and firewalls

- The strategic installation of intrusion detection systems and firewalls fortifies networks against external attacks.

- Firewalls: Acting as dynamic gatekeepers, firewalls keep an eye on and regulate network traffic in accordance with pre-established security regulations, thus thwarting potential cyber invasions and unauthorized access.

- Intrusion Detection Systems (IDS): By utilizing sophisticated anomaly detection algorithms, IDS actively improves the overall security posture by quickly identifying and mitigating potential security risks.

4. The encryption process:

The use of encryption protocols elevates the field of information security to new heights.

- Application of Cryptography: Using cryptographic techniques to convert sensitive data into ciphertext and protect information while it's being sent or stored.

- Quantum-Resistant Encryption: The incorporation of quantum-resistant encryption techniques becomes essential for long-term digital defense in response to new threats.

5. Security Guidelines and Protocols

- The creation and execution of thorough security policies and procedures are essential to the building of a robust security posture.

- Governance, Risk Management, and Compliance (GRC): Using cutting-edge GRC solutions to oversee security frameworks, which include compliance standards, best practices, and protocols to help firms achieve strong security.

6. Training and Awareness of Security:

- Basic security includes the vital human component in addition to technical safeguards.

- Cultivation of Security Awareness: Encouraging users to adopt a security-aware mindset so they can identify possible threats and take appropriate action.

- Ongoing Training Initiatives: Giving people access to cutting-edge tools and methods for ongoing instruction and training, enabling them to traverse the digital terrain with increased awareness.

7. Patch Administration:

- A proactive approach to patch management is necessary due to the changing nature of the digital ecosystem.

- Automated Solutions: Making use of sophisticated automated solutions powered by AI-driven vulnerability scanners, which guarantee that software and systems are regularly updated and patched to quickly fix identified vulnerabilities.

This thorough overview of fundamental security concepts establishes the foundation for a strong defense against the numerous threats presented by the digital frontier. Following these guidelines becomes crucial as people and organizations attempt to manage the complexity of the digital world. This will protect digital assets' availability, confidentiality, and integrity against ever-changing cyber threats.

CHAPTER FOUR

4.0 Penetrating: Getting Around the Cybersecurity Environment

Penetration testing is a dynamic and essential process that is purposefully designed to enhance digital defenses against a wide range of potential attacks in the constantly changing field of cybersecurity. This part explores the principles of penetration testing in great detail, going into great detail about it. We peel back the layers that make penetration testing a vital instrument in the fight for cyber resilience, from definition and methods to the critical role of ethical hackers.

4.1 Explanation of Penetration Testing

1. Determining the Scope of Penetration Testing: Fundamentally, *Penetration Testing* consists of permitted and controlled cyberattack simulations carried out on systems, networks, or applications. This proactive strategy, which is sometimes confused with ethical hacking or white-hat hacking, tries to find and take advantage of vulnerabilities before malevolent actors can do so. Penetration testing is a tactical tool used to continuously improve cybersecurity defenses by putting oneself in the shoes of possible adversaries.

2. Consent and Authorization: The specific authorization and approval gained from the entity or organization responsible for the system under review is a crucial premise that guides penetration testing. Penetration testers who are ethical hackers stay inside pre-established parameters and make sure their actions follow moral and legal guidelines. The focus on openness sets penetration testing apart from malevolent hacking and encourages a cooperative and moral search for improved security.

3. The Penetration Testers' Role: Penetration testers who are also ethical hackers play a crucial part in the cybersecurity environment. Equipped with an in-depth knowledge of hacking methods, tools, and strategies, they imitate cyberattacks in order to find weaknesses that might evade conventional security measures. Organizations can improve their overall security posture by proactively addressing and remediating possible gaps with the knowledge gained from penetration tests.

Methodologies in Penetration Testing:

The methodical approach of penetration testing consists of multiple phases, each of which adds to a thorough evaluation of the security posture of an organization.

- Reconnaissance: Compiling extensive data about the system or network of interest.

- Scanning: Actively exploring to find live hosts, open ports, and services.

- Enumeration: Gathering more data on the target to improve comprehension of possible weaknesses.

- Exploitation: Making active attempts to take advantage of vulnerabilities found in order to imitate actual cyberthreats.

- Post-Exploitation Analysis: Assessing the effects of successful exploits and locating potential new vulnerabilities, offering a comprehensive assessment of possible hazards.

5. technologies of the Trade: To properly replicate a wide spectrum of cyber threats, ethical hackers conducting penetration testing use a sophisticated and varied array of technologies.

- Network Scanners: Locating open ports and security holes in the target system.

- Exploitation Frameworks: Identifying and exploiting vulnerabilities automatically.

- Password Cracking Tools: Improving overall access control, evaluating the robustness of authentication systems.

- Wireless Testing Tools: Assessing the organization's wireless networks' security.

- Web Application Scanners: Recognizing vulnerabilities unique to web apps, an essential part of contemporary digital environments.

6. Accountability and Suggestions:
Thorough reporting of results and suggestions is a vital component of penetration testing. Ethical hackers carefully record vulnerabilities they find, their possible effects on the company, and suggestions for remedy. Organizations are able to prioritize and effectively resolve vulnerabilities thanks to this precise information, which promotes a proactive and flexible approach to cybersecurity.

7. Ongoing Education and Adjustment:
Because penetration testing is an intrinsically dynamic field, it calls for constant learning and adjustment. By doing this, ethical hackers keep up with the most recent developments in defensive technologies, hacking methodologies, and upcoming vulnerabilities. The dedication to continuous learning guarantees penetration testing's continued effectiveness and relevance among the always changing cyber threat environment.

To sum up, the practice of penetration testing is essential to achieving strong cybersecurity. It is not only useful but also essential for enterprises to have a thorough understanding of the concepts and procedures of penetration testing as they traverse the complexity of the digital realm. By using penetration testing, ethical hacking helps identify and mitigate potential vulnerabilities, which in turn helps build a strong cybersecurity posture against new and existing cyber threats.

4.2 Real-World Use: Detailed Step-by-Step Guide to Penetration Testing

Putting penetration testing into practice is a complex process that calls for a methodical and thorough strategy to thoroughly evaluate and strengthen digital defenses. We will explore the nuances of carrying out a penetration test in this extensive and detailed step-by-step tutorial. This guide is to offer an extensive road map for ethical hackers and cybersecurity experts involved in the crucial duty of detecting vulnerabilities and improving overall cyber resilience, from the first phases of preparation to the complexities of post-exploitation research.

1. Planning Stage: Outlining Goals and Extent

- Definitive Objective: The planning stage starts with a precise description of the penetration tester's goals. Setting clear goals for the testing process guarantees a targeted and efficient investigation, regardless of the aim: evaluating the security of a particular application, network, or system as a whole.

- Scope Determination: Determine the systems, networks, or applications that will be evaluated in order to define the penetration tester's scope. Setting limits is essential to ensuring ethical and approved testing, and getting the appropriate parties' express consent is crucial.

- Rules of Engagement: Make sure that everyone participating, including the internal personnel and ethical hackers, is aware of the rules of engagement. To prevent misconceptions during the testing process, this involves specifying precise testing procedures, deadlines, and any limitations.

- Documentation and Project Charter: Create a thorough project charter and documentation that includes the goals, rules of participation, and other pertinent information. This documentation acts as a fundamental point of reference throughout the duration of the penetration testing procedure.

2. Reconnaissance: Information Gathering

- Passive Reconnaissance: Gather data about the target system or network without engaging with it directly to start the reconnaissance phase. Investigating publicly accessible data, such as company websites, social media profiles, or domain registration details, may be necessary for this.

- Active Reconnaissance: Make the switch to active reconnaissance by looking for services, open ports, and live hosts on the target. One can use programs such as Nmap to find possible points of entry for additional investigation.

- Enumeration: Use enumeration to obtain further details about the target, including network shares, user accounts, and system configurations. One important stage in locating potential flaws and vulnerabilities is enumeration.

- Information Gathering Tools: To improve the reconnaissance process, use a range of information gathering tools, including WHOIS databases, DNS interrogation tools, and social engineering strategies. The more thorough the data collected, the more accurately the penetration test can mimic actual cyberthreats.

3. Scanning: Finding Weaknesses

- Vulnerability Scanning: Check the target for known vulnerabilities using automated tools such as Nessus, OpenVAS, or Qualys. This stage offers a thorough rundown of potential flaws that knowledgeable hackers can investigate further.

- Network Mapping: Make a thorough map of the target network, noting the connections between various systems and possible avenues through which an intruder might gain access. Mapping intricate network topologies can be made easier with the use of visualization tools like Maltego.

- Network and Service Enumeration: Complete a thorough enumeration of network services, noting configurations and version numbers. This data helps ethical hackers customize their strategy for the exploitation stage.

- Wireless Network Scanning: To find weaknesses in wireless infrastructure, if applicable, carry out wireless network scanning. To evaluate the security of wireless networks, one can use programs such as Wireshark or Aircrack-ng.

4. Exploitation: Cyber Attack Simulation

- Tool Selection: - Select the right tools to take advantage of vulnerabilities that have been found. Ethical hackers can mimic actual cyberattacks by utilizing a variety of flaws available in popular frameworks like Metasploit.

- Gaining Access: Try to use security holes in systems or networks to obtain unauthorized access. This stage imitates the strategies employed by malevolent hackers, enabling ethical hackers to spot possible gaps in security protocols.

- Privilege Escalation: Examine methods for obtaining greater levels of access within the intended environment by utilizing privilege escalation. Ethical hackers use a simulation of privilege escalation to find possible holes in access controls.

- Web Application Exploitation: Pay attention to web application exploitation if it applies. Use tools such as Burp Suite or OWASP ZAP to find and take advantage of web application vulnerabilities that mirror actual cyberthreats.

5. Analysis of Post-Exploitation: Assessing Impact

- Assessing Impact: Take into account the possible repercussions of a breach while assessing the impact of successful exploits. This entails determining the degree of access obtained, compromising sensitive data, or possible system damage.

- Pivoting: Use the first access obtained to investigate additional avenues for exploitation. Ethical hackers can navigate laterally through a network by pivoting, finding new weak spots and possible entry points.

- Simulation of Data Exfiltration: Evaluate the efficacy of data protection mechanisms by simulating data exfiltration scenarios. The goal of ethical hackers is to find and fix any potential gaps in privacy and data security protocols.

6. Reporting and Suggestions: Sharing Results

- Documentation: Thoroughly document every finding, including vulnerabilities found, exploits that work, and any possible effects on the target environment. Give a thorough and in-depth summary of the penetration test by clearly articulating the processes that were followed.

- Risk Prioritization: Sort vulnerabilities that have been found according to their seriousness and possible influence on the company. By setting priorities, stakeholders can efficiently manage cyber risks by concentrating on resolving the most pressing concerns first.

- Remedial Suggestions: Offer thorough remediation advice that specify how to resolve and lessen vulnerabilities that have been found. Organizations are empowered to improve their security posture by using these practical recommendations.

- Executive Summary: Write an executive summary that succinctly informs leadership and non-technical stakeholders of the main conclusions, risks, and suggested courses of action. A high-level overview of the penetration test results is given in this report.

7. Ongoing Education and Development: Changing Security Posture

- Debriefing: Have a thorough debriefing session with stakeholders to go over the conclusions, revelations, and lessons discovered during the penetration test. This cooperative conversation improves security procedures and tactics.

- Update Security Measures: Apply required security patches, updates, and configurations in accordance with the guidelines given. To keep abreast of emerging cyber threats, security measures should be updated and improved on a regular basis.

- Continuous Training: Continually teach internal staff members to improve their knowledge of potential security risks and cybersecurity best practices. Having a knowledgeable staff is essential to keeping a strong security posture.

- Documentation Review: Make sure that all documentation pertaining to the penetration test is kept up to date and pertinent by periodically reviewing and updating it. Future testing and efforts at continuous improvement can benefit greatly from the use of documentation.

Organizations can proactively detect and resolve vulnerabilities by carefully adhering to this thorough and detailed step-by-step guide to the practical application of penetration testing. This will ultimately promote a strong and resilient cybersecurity posture in the face of a constantly changing digital landscape.

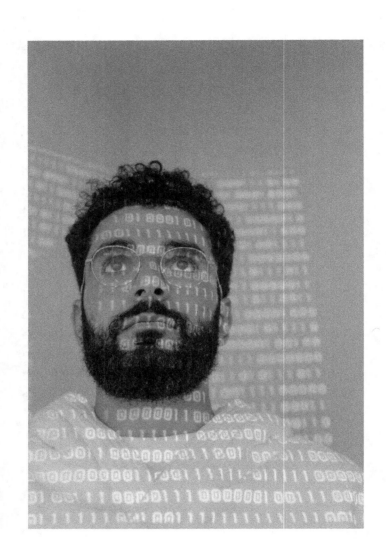

CHAPTER FIVE

5.1 Getting Ahead in the Depths with Cybersecurity Essentials: A Comprehensive Look

Gaining a thorough understanding of cybersecurity's fundamentals is not only advantageous but also critical for people and organizations who want to safely navigate the digital world. "Digital Defense Essential" adopts a direct approach, breaking down complex ideas into easily understood insights. This long section attempts to give readers a thorough and comprehensive overview of the major subjects covered in the book, giving them an in-depth and approachable introduction to the diverse field of cybersecurity.

1. Establishing the Groundwork: Clarifying Fundamental Ideas

- Elucidating the Threat Environment: To start, we explore the many layers of the threat landscape and the nuances of various cyberthreats. From the nuances of ransomware and social engineering to the complexities of malware and phishing, this section offers invaluable insights that equip readers with the knowledge they need to manage potential risks.

- Simplifying Risk Handling: In terms of risk management, the book streamlines the complex procedures related to analyzing and reducing cybersecurity risks. Readers obtain thorough understanding of recognizing, assessing, and ranking risks, encouraging a proactive and tactical approach to cybersecurity.

2. Putting Practicable Security Measures in Place: Effectiveness-Based Strategies

- Password Security Proficiency: Addressing the pervasive problem of password security, the book skillfully instructs readers on creating strong, one-of-a-kind passwords and putting secure password management procedures into place. It also emphasizes the significance of multi-factor authentication as an extra line of protection.

- Tactics for Strategic Endpoint Security: We also apply a practical approach to endpoint security, where readers receive not only information but also guidance regarding the importance of safeguarding devices. Practical advice is liberally offered for putting into practice efficient endpoint protection measures, including antivirus software, device encryption, and the frequent installation of software updates.

3. Protecting Digital Boundaries: A Comprehensive Examination of Network Security

- Understanding Firewalls: The book carefully dissects the principles of these digital gatekeepers, demystifying the crucial role that firewalls play in network defense and giving readers a sophisticated grasp of how they function and their vital role in blocking malicious activity and preventing unauthorized access.

- Basic Intruder Detection: The book introduces readers to the principles of intrusion detection systems, enabling them to not only recognize but also take proactive measures in response to potential security threats. - The frequently perceived complexity of intrusion detection is laid bare in a simplified manner.

4. Strengthening Digital Assets: Comprehensive Data Security Techniques

- Exploring the Cryptocurrency Domain: A useful investigation takes place, illuminating encryption and its critical function in protecting confidential information. The reader is taken through the process by which encryption converts data into an unintelligible format, enhancing data confidentiality both in transit and storage.

- A Comprehensive Method for Safe Data Management: The book emphasizes secure data handling procedures and gives readers a plethora of useful advice on safeguarding confidential data. From careful data disposal to secure file storage, key tactics are laid out in a way that is not only understandable but also actively applicable.

5. Handling Cybersecurity Issues in a Proactive Way: An Incident Response Framework

- Readiness for Online Disasters: Recognizing that cybersecurity incidents are inevitable, the book acts as a guide to help readers not only plan ahead for incidents but also effectively respond to them. It provides detailed information on practical incident response strategies that enable individuals and organizations to reduce the impact of security breaches.

- Taking Insights from Actual Situations: Through the integration of real-world scenarios and case studies, the book provides readers with valuable insights into real-world cybersecurity challenges. Through the analysis of documented incidents, readers are able to gain a tangible and practical understanding of potential threats and effective strategies for responding to them.

6. Fostering Cyber Resilience: An All-encompassing Perspective on Security Awareness Culture

- Recognizing the Human Factor: Acknowledging the critical role that people play in cybersecurity, the book highlights the need for a security-aware culture. Readers are not only aided in developing a proactive security mindset among users, but are also given the tools they need to create a strong defense against phishing and social engineering attacks.

- Education for Ongoing Vigilance: The book offers a roadmap for implementing security awareness training, so that individuals in an organization are not only aware of the evolving threats to their organization, but are also prepared to respond to them. This is an example of how the practical approach to security awareness extends to training programs.

"Digital Defense Essential" is a methodical approach to learning the foundational concepts of cybersecurity. Whether you are a beginner looking to grasp the fundamentals or an experienced professional in need of real-world knowledge, this book is a comprehensive and invaluable tool for improving cybersecurity knowledge in an organized, comprehensible, and useful way.

5.2 A Thorough Step-by-Step Manual for Cybersecurity Expertise: Developing Digital Hardiness

In the dynamic field of cybersecurity, mastery requires a methodical, systematic, and sequential approach. "Digital Defense Essential" presents a comprehensive road map for individuals and organizations seeking to strengthen their digital resilience. It covers fundamental ideas, realistic security precautions, network defense plans, and incident response techniques. It provides readers with a thorough and comprehensive introduction to the complex world of cybersecurity.

Step 1: Establishing the Base - Comprehending Fundamental Ideas

- Explore the Threat Environment: Getting Through the Cyber Maze: Start this fundamental step by learning about the complex web of threats that define the digital sphere. Investigate the various aspects of cyber threats, ranging from the cunning ways that malware operates to the skillful ways that social engineering operates. This study serves as the cornerstone of your cybersecurity adventure, offering you a sophisticated knowledge of the ever-changing and dynamic challenges that lie ahead in the digital abyss.

  As you work through the complexities of the threat landscape, realize how important it is to stay up to date on new threats. This understanding establishes a strong base and gives you the tools you need to confidently and resiliently navigate the complexities of cybersecurity. As you explore, the understanding that cyber threats are dynamic acts as a compass for you as you venture into the world of digital defense.

- Simplify Risk Management: Handling Uncertainty's Waters: Continue your journey by navigating the waters of uncertainty with a thorough exploration of risk management processes. Develop your skills in risk assessment and mitigation techniques, creating a strong framework that enables you to accurately anticipate and respond to potential threats. Master the art of identifying, evaluating, and prioritizing risks to establish a proactive and strategic approach to cybersecurity.

  Recognize that risk mitigation and threat landscape understanding go hand in hand as you streamline risk management. This coordinated approach strengthens your cybersecurity efforts and provides a strong basis for proactive defense in the dynamic digital landscape.

Step 2: Put into Practice Useful Security Measures - Effectiveness Strategies

- Secure Digital Gateways using Master Passwords: In this critical step, you will learn how to master password security. You will go beyond strength to create passwords that are distinctly strong. You will also learn about secure password management practices and how important they are to digital defense. You will also learn about the importance of multi-factor authentication and how it provides an extra layer of protection against unauthorized access. Finally, you will strengthen your digital gateways by mastering password security strategically.

- Implement Endpoint Protection Strategies: Protecting Digital Frontiers: Expand your knowledge of digital defense by putting into practice thorough device security measures. Learn about endpoint security strategies and cover important topics like antivirus software, device encryption, and software updates on a regular basis.

Make sure your digital perimeters are protected against possible cyberattacks. This step creates a strong defense system that protects endpoints from the ever-changing world of digital vulnerabilities.

Step 3: Protect Digital Boundaries: An Extensive Exploration of Network Security

- Cracking Firewalls: Becoming Experts at the Keepers of Digital Gates: Gain a deep comprehension of the critical role firewalls play in network defense. Learn the nuances of how firewalls function as watchful sentinels, blocking unwanted access and thwarting malicious activity. Boost your expertise by learning how to configure and maintain firewalls for maximum security. In this step, you will discover the keys to becoming an expert in firewall management, positioning them as powerful defenders of digital gates.

- Take the Complexity Out of Intrusion Detection: Learn more about intrusion detection systems as you make your way through the complex world of network security. Arm yourself with the knowledge to not only identify possible security threats but also to take precise action in response to them. Become an expert in intrusion detection, which will help you improve the security posture of your network infrastructure overall. This step puts you in the forefront of protecting digital perimeters, where intrusion detection expertise is essential to strong network defense.

Step 4: Handle Cybersecurity Issues - A Preemptive Method for Incident Handling

- Strengthening Defenses to Prepare for Cyber Incidents: Recognize that cybersecurity incidents are inevitable and bolster your defenses with well-thought-out plans for effective responses. Create and improve all-encompassing incident response strategies to reduce the impact of security breaches. In this step, make sure that there is a prompt and well-coordinated response that not only resolves the current issue but also improves your cybersecurity posture as a whole.

- Take Insights from Actual Situations: Acquiring Knowledge from Experience: In this step, utilize the abundance of experiences from real-world incidents to improve your ability to navigate cybersecurity challenges proactively. Immerse yourself in the practical application of knowledge by integrating case studies and real-world scenarios. Gain insightful understanding of actual cybersecurity challenges, enabling the application of lessons learned in diverse contexts.

Step 5: Fostering Cyber Resilience - An All-encompassing Perspective on Security Awareness Culture

- Embracing Cyber Guardians: Recognizing the Human Element: In this step, you will acknowledge the human element as a powerful force in the cybersecurity landscape and begin the process of nurturing cyber guardians. Acknowledge the critical role that the human element plays in cybersecurity and set out to create a culture that empowers individuals within an organization to actively contribute to a resilient defense against social engineering and phishing attacks.

- Develop Cyber Sentinel Skills to Maintain Constant Vigilance: Develop cyber sentinel skills that enable people to become proactive defenders, fostering a culture of continuous vigilance. In this step, develop training that becomes the cornerstone of a resilient defense, where every member of the organization contributes to the collective strength against cyber threats. In this way, you can extend the practical approach to security awareness through the implementation of effective training programs.

Set out on this thorough, step-by-step journey to become a cybersecurity master, laying a solid foundation and honing the skills necessary to confidently traverse the complex world of digital security. Each step is more than just a task; it's an immersive experience that has been thoughtfully designed to offer a systematic, all-encompassing, and game-changing method that will enable people and organizations to effectively strengthen their cybersecurity defenses.

- Easily Gliding Through the Depths of Cybersecurity Fundamentals: A Comprehensive Examination for a Smooth Understanding: Understanding the basics comes first in our quest for cybersecurity expertise. "Digital Defense Essentials" is a comprehensive section that is thoughtfully crafted to shed light on key ideas that serve as the foundation for a solid understanding of cybersecurity. This in-depth analysis goes beyond superficial definitions, seeking to provide readers with a deep and approachable introduction to the complexities of cybersecurity.

5.3 Comprehending Fundamental Ideas - Bringing the Complex to Light

Disclosing Details and Demystifying the Threat Landscape

Take a thorough tour to discover the many strands that make up the threat landscape. This section goes beyond simple definitions, exploring the nuances of different cyberthreats. By dissecting these threats, readers acquire not only knowledge but also a sophisticated comprehension of the difficulties that arise in the ever-changing digital space. In this section, we shed light on the intricate, giving readers a profound understanding of the constantly changing threat landscape.

Risk Landscape Navigation: Comprehensive Risk Management

Go deeply into the field of risk management, stressing a comprehensive comprehension of its procedures. This section traverses the terrain of recognizing, assessing, and ranking risks, cultivating a deep understanding of the proactive and strategic approach necessary to manage cybersecurity risks successfully. We lead readers through the complex process of navigating risks in this section, guaranteeing that they acquire a thorough understanding of cybersecurity risk management.

Building Digital Fortresses: Developing the Art of Password Proficiency

Improve your knowledge of password security by learning how to create strong, long-lasting passwords. This section offers advice as well as insights into safe password management techniques, emphasizing the critical role that multi-factor authentication plays in improving overall digital defense. We also walk readers through building digital fortifications through password mastery, making sure they have the skills necessary to protect their digital identities.

Defining Endpoint Security Strategies: Digital Fortifications Simplicity

This section explains the complexities of endpoint security, enabling readers to navigate the digital landscape with a heightened sense of security. Advance further by putting clear and effective measures for securing digital endpoints into place. From antivirus software to device encryption, this segment simplifies the intricacies of endpoint security tactics.

Adding Light to Firewall Principles: Going Beyond the Surface

Provide readers with a clear path to comprehending and putting into practice effective network defense by shedding light on the role of firewalls in network defense and delving deeper into their functions and significance. This section breaks down the configuration and management of firewalls and walks readers through the fundamentals of strengthening digital perimeters with real-world examples.

Navigating Threat Terrain: Mastering Intrusion Detection with Simplicity

Handle the intricacy of intrusion detection systems with ease. This section breaks down the comprehension of how these systems identify and react to security threats, enabling readers to become proficient in the art of intrusion detection for improved network security. In this section, we walk readers through the process of becoming proficient in intrusion detection in a straightforward manner, guaranteeing they have the know-how to protect digital perimeters from constantly changing threats.

Breaking Down Encryption: Providing Light on Data Security

Explain the complex world of encryption and how important it is to protect sensitive data. This section goes beyond definitions to show readers how encryption improves data confidentiality during transmission and storage. We also explain the fundamentals of encryption so that readers can understand how important it is to protect digital assets in an easy-to-understand manner.

Adopting a Comprehensive Method for Data Management: Maintaining Security Simplicity

In this section, we walk readers through adopting a holistic approach to data handling and provide them with useful insights for protecting digital assets. We also simplify the intricacies of secure file storage and careful data disposal, so readers can put strategies that protect sensitive information throughout its lifecycle into practice with ease.

Effective Incident Management - Transitioning
from Intricacy to Readiness

Simplifying Preparedness: Essentials of Incident Response

Recognize that cybersecurity incidents are inevitable and be ready to respond appropriately. This section breaks down the essentials of incident response so readers can easily understand them and develop proactive strategies to reduce the impact of security breaches. With this in hand, readers will be better equipped to handle the challenges presented by the ever-changing cybersecurity landscape.

Practical Application and Real-World Insights: Linking Theory and Practice

In this section, we bridge theory and practice, giving readers real-world insights for effective incident response. We do this by drawing lessons from real-world scenarios, moving beyond theoretical concepts to practical application. We also integrate practical insights into cybersecurity challenges, enabling readers to apply lessons learned in diverse contexts and ensuring readiness for the constantly changing cybersecurity landscape.

Handling Cybersecurity Awareness While Simplifying the Human Element

This section covers cybersecurity awareness, making sure readers understand the importance of the human element in maintaining a secure digital environment. It also simplifies the development of a security-aware culture and empowers individuals to actively contribute to a resilient defense against social engineering and phishing attacks.

Convenient Vigilance Training: Connecting Information and Implementation

In this segment, we bridge knowledge and action by offering readers user-friendly training for effective cybersecurity resilience. We also simplify the process of empowering people with the knowledge and skills necessary to not only recognize but actively respond to evolving cyber threats proactively, fostering a culture of continuous vigilance. Increase the practical application of security awareness with user-friendly training programs.

"Digital Defense Essentials" is a thorough guide that illuminates the way to grasp fundamental ideas with ease. Every section is designed to go beyond cursory explanations and create an atmosphere where readers can confidently and easily traverse the complex terrain of cybersecurity.

CONCLUSION

Essential Ideas for Cybersecurity Proficiency

The last section, "Conclusion: Recapitulating Key Concepts," provides a summary of the most important topics we have covered thus far in this thorough guide to cybersecurity. This final section provides readers with a succinct summary of the main ideas, perceptions, and tactics discussed, enabling them to better comprehend and take charge of their cybersecurity activities.

A Recapitulation of Key Concepts: Summarizing the Journey

Understanding Cybersecurity Fundamentals: Summarize the key ideas discussed, from comprehending the fundamental security measures to demystifying the threat landscape. This section emphasizes how important it is to understand fundamental ideas in order to have a solid basis for cybersecurity.

How to Handle a Career in Security:
Think back on the knowledge you've received about the variety of career options in cybersecurity. Provide a brief overview of the investigation of specialized positions, career pathways, and tactics for ongoing development in the ever-changing cybersecurity labor market.

Practical Advice for Career growth:
Re-examine the practical guidance on career growth, advancing into cybersecurity, developing a personal brand for long-term success, and mastering soft skills from seasoned experts.

Creating a Prosperous Career in the Cybersecurity Sector:
Apply the techniques described to create a prosperous career in the cybersecurity sector. Provide a brief summary of the key elements of long-term professional development, including strategic planning, ongoing education, efficient networking, and striking a balance between hard and soft abilities.

A Last Word on Strengthening the Cybersecurity Journey

To sum up, this guide has been designed to be a thorough companion for people and businesses navigating the complex world of cybersecurity. The ideas and tactics shared are meant to support your journey, regardless of your level of experience. If you are a novice looking to lay a strong foundation, an aspiring professional planning your career path, or an experienced practitioner seeking ongoing improvement.

The main lessons from this guide act as guiding lights as the cybersecurity environment changes. Develop an attitude of perpetual learning, accept the changing character of the industry, and participate actively in the cybersecurity community. Your position is crucial in the cybersecurity ecosystem, whether it is protecting digital perimeters, responding to incidents, or advancing the profession.

Understanding cybersecurity is more than simply a set of skills in the ever-growing digital world; it's a dedication to protecting the digital space. May the information you acquire here operate as a springboard for success, resiliency, and a long-lasting influence on the security of the digital world as you begin or continue your cybersecurity path.

Support for Future Cybersecurity Fans: Developing Your Route to Digital Defender: This section serves as a rallying cry and a lighthouse of encouragement for aspiring cybersecurity aficionados entering the fascinating field of digital defense. It will help you navigate the thrilling adventure that lies ahead. Remember that your quest of cybersecurity expertise is a commitment to safeguarding the digital world as well as a career as you set out to become a defender of the digital frontier. The following quotes will inspire you and strengthen your resolve:

Adopt the Learning Journey: In the field of cybersecurity, one's journey is an ongoing quest for understanding, as information truly is power. Accept the excitement of learning, from identifying intricate risks to being proficient with state-of-the-art technologies. Savor the thrill of solving the puzzles around the digital world, as each new finding propels your development into a strong cybersecurity expert.

Overcome Obstacles with Perseverance: There are difficulties on the path you have selected. The dynamic field of cybersecurity necessitates resilience in the face of ever changing threats. Every obstacle you face presents a chance for you to get stronger. Take a tenacious approach to obstacles because it's only by conquering them that your abilities and knowledge will grow.

Build an Inquisitive Mentality: In the constantly evolving field of cybersecurity, your best ally is curiosity. Develop an attitude that is always open to understanding, asking questions, and exploring. Your unquenchable curiosity will distinguish you and help you reach new heights in your path as you explore further into security concepts and technologies.

Create a Peer and Mentor Network: On this trip, you are not by yourself. Make connections with other enthusiasts, participate in conversations, and create a network of like-minded individuals. Seek the guidance of seasoned professionals who may offer you advice and insights as a mentor. The cybersecurity community is a sizable and encouraging ecosystem that is prepared to foster your development.

Build Practical Skills: While theory establishes the groundwork, competence is attained via actual skills. Participate in practical experiences through real-world projects, labs, or simulations. Applying your knowledge to real-world situations improves your problem-solving abilities and makes you a skilled cybersecurity practitioner.

Remain Up to Date in a Changing Environment: Like the digital environment, you have to be constantly evolving. Keep up with new developments in defense tactics, threats, and technology. Engage in active participation in online networks, conferences, and forums to stay on the cutting edge of the cybersecurity industry.

Appreciate Your Advancement: Celebrate each and every accomplishment, no matter how tiny. Whether it's finishing a difficult project, obtaining a certification, or landing a great internship, every accomplishment advances you. Enjoy your accomplishments and channel them into inspiration for the next leg of your trip.

Show Your Passion to Others: As you travel the cybersecurity route, allow your enthusiasm to serve as an example for others. Talk to others, impart your knowledge, and help the community learn more as a whole. You have the ability to pique the interest of other enthusiasts with your excitement.

Keep in Mind the Difference You Can Make: Your work in cybersecurity protects the fundamental structure of our digital civilization; it goes beyond codes and algorithms. Recall the impact that data protection, network security, and cyber threat defense may have. Your efforts are significant and have an impact that goes well beyond the code you create.

The path ahead may be difficult, but if you use resolve as your guide, you can gracefully negotiate the complexity of cybersecurity. Driven by your fervor and dedication to safeguarding the digital realm, march forward. You make a contribution to the global landscape's collective resilience with every step you take.

Know that your passion and commitment are what will keep you moving forward as you set out on this exciting journey into the broad and dynamic field of cybersecurity. As a digital defender, you play a critical role whose influence will be seen in the security and robustness of our digital future. Remember that the cybersecurity community appreciates and encourages your contribution as you embrace the challenges and celebrate your successes. I hope your path is one of growth, discovery, and the satisfaction that comes from protecting the digital sphere. Cheers to your exploration!

www.ingramcontent.com/pod-product-compliance
Lightning Source LLC
La Vergne TN
LVHW051327050326
832903LV00031B/3401